CREATING A HOME

DESIGNING AND PLANNING
DINING AREAS

WARD LOCK

For the Mistress
of Mulecroft Brow.
20/7/99
Happy planning
Happy hunting
Happy life with
Happy dining.
David
xx

CONTENTS

A WARD LOCK BOOK

First published in the UK in 1997
by Ward Lock, Wellington House, 125 Strand,
London WC2R 0BB

A Cassell imprint

Copyright © Eaglemoss Publications Ltd 1997
Based on *Creating a Home*
Copyright © cover design Ward Lock 1997

All rights reserved

Distributed in Australia
by New Holland Publishers Pty Ltd, 3/2 Aquatic Drive,
Frenchs Forest, NSW, Australia 2086

Distributed in Canada
by Cavendish Books Inc., Unit 5, 801 West 1st Street,
North Vancouver, B.C. Canada V7P 1PH

A British Library Cataloguing in Publication Data block for
this book may be obtained from the British Library

ISBN 0 7063 7658 7
Printed in Spain by Cayfosa Industria Grafica
10 9 8 7 6 5 4 3 2

INTRODUCTION

To do justice to a carefully prepared meal, whether it is served to the family or to invited guests, you need room to savour it in style and comfort. **Designing and Planning Dining Areas** tells you all you need to know about making dining at home a pleasure, whether you have a kitchen-diner, eat in a corner of the living room, or enjoy the luxury of a separate dining room.

Assessing your needs is the key to successful planning, and this book helps you consider all the options to avoid what could prove to be costly mistakes. The first few chapters emphasize practical questions such as comfort and convenience, and help you choose the best location for your dining area, select the furniture you need, and get the lighting right. Diagrams and floor plans illustrate precisely how much space you need and how to make the best use of it.

The way you decorate a dining area plays a large part in creating the right atmosphere for both family meals and dinner parties. The centre section of this book is lavishly illustrated with dining areas of every possible style, size and shape. There are dining rooms in a variety of styles, both traditional and modern, alongside others designed to double up as family rooms. Combined living room and kitchen-diners are covered in detail and you will find plenty of bright ideas for simple dividers and space-saving furniture to help ease the squeeze.

Further chapters present different room schemes with captions highlighting the main features that make them work – from country house to city-slick kitchen-diners and a Victorian-style dining room which draws on the past for inspiration.

The final chapters present an illustrated guide to everything you need to buy to furnish and equip a dining area, advising on the bewildering choice of tables and dining chairs (both modern and traditional), serving tables and trolleys, glassware, china and cutlery.

Designing and Planning Dining Areas is an essential book of ideas for anyone setting up home for the first time, moving into a new home or just in the mood for redecoration.

Room to Dine

In today's smaller homes and with the busy lifestyle of most families, it is tempting to neglect the dining area and make do with a table in the kitchen or living room. Even if the whole family eats together only once a week and you entertain rarely, it is worth making your dining area comfortable.

Eating should be an enjoyable experience, a time for families to gather at least once a day. Balancing a tray on your lap in front of the television, or making do with a breakfast bar is no way to enjoy food – it also destroys the social aspect of family meals.

There's no need to go overboard for a formal separate dining room – unless, of course, your lifestyle includes regular entertaining. Most family dining rooms can double for other uses, such as study, letter writing or homework, or with the addition of a sofa bed, become an extra guest room. Alternatively, you can establish a dining area in the kitchen, in a conservatory or at one end of the living room.

SITING THE DINING ROOM
For maximum convenience, the dining room should be close to the kitchen, preferably connected by a serving hatch so that crockery and hot dishes need not be carried any distance.

Existing dining room Is it in the right place and do you really use it? If the room is inconvenient and under-used, think about making better use of the space, as a study perhaps, or as a family room. Eating can be moved to a kitchen diner, or into a conservatory.

Kitchen/diner For many families, a kitchen/diner is the best solution to the space problem. Try to screen the area from the main part of the kitchen. You can do this by installing a counter with storage beneath between the cooking and eating areas (it can double as a breakfast bar), or, if there isn't enough space for a counter, a low wall. A ceiling-mounted venetian or roller blind can be pulled down to wall level so that diners can't see into the kitchen – few cooks enjoy being watched at work.

Living room/diner Modern through rooms where a central dividing wall has been removed often have a dining area at the end nearest the kitchen. If possible, make a hatchway through to the kitchen to make serving and clearing easier.

Ventilation Try to site the dining area near a window which can be opened to disperse smoke and food smells. In the kitchen, an extractor fan positioned above the cooker helps.

△ **Custom-built dining**
This cleverly designed dining area is divided from the kitchen by open shelving which doubles as a serving hatch.

BRIGHT IDEA

Make a fold-down table A simple fold-down table top (which can be used with folding chairs) is a space-saving way to add a dining area to the kitchen.

To make the top, fix wooden battens to the wall, as shown right. Hinge a length of laminate-covered or wood kitchen worktop to the battens, then attach folding hinges to the underside. Folding hinges which come in a variety of sizes are available from good DIY and hardware stores.

ROOM TO MOVE

People need elbow and leg room and enough space to get in and out.

Elbow room Each person needs about 60cm (2ft) of space when sitting at a table on a chair without arms. If the chair has arms, add 5cm (2in) each side.

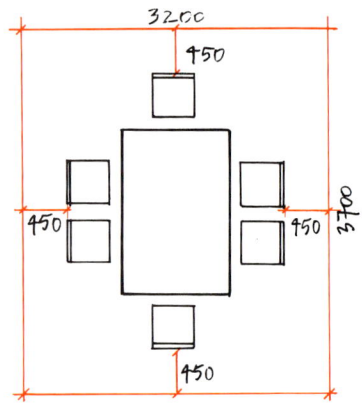

△ *Rectangular setting for six*

Leg room There should be enough leg room for the average adult to get his or her legs under the table with ease. As a general rule, the chair seat should be 25cm (10in) from the top of the table.

Getting in and out It is annoying and uncomfortable if people have to climb over one another to get to or leave the table. Ideally, there should be 45-60cm

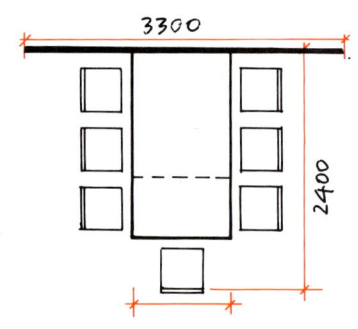

△ *Wall-mounted table for seven*

(1ft 6in-2ft) of space behind the chair so that it can be pushed away from the table and allow enough space for the person using it to stand up.

If lack of space means you must have fixed bench dining seating which cannot be moved, make sure you choose a table which isn't too heavy to be pushed out of the way.

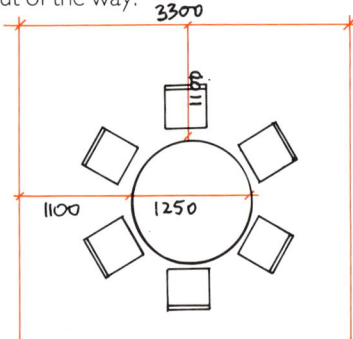

△ *Round setting for six*

BUYING DINING FURNITURE

First make a plan of the room, marking doors, windows, radiators and furniture you want to keep. List the following and take the list with you.

Table size What is the biggest size table the room can accommodate comfortably? Buying a table which extends to a large size makes no sense if the room is too small for it to be used to full capacity. When buying a table with an extension, ask to see the table with the extension in place. On some tables, the legs stay in the same place when the extension is inserted – usually right where they will restrict leg movement.

Table shape Dining tables come in round, oval, square and rectangular shapes. In a small room, a round or oval table is less visually restricting than a rectangular table – and you won't bump your hips on the corners. To work out the number of people the table can seat, measure sides and ends or the circumference of the table then divide the measurement by 60cm (2ft) which is the average amount of space needed per person.

Number of chairs Work out how many chairs are needed for daily use and how many for guests. Folding chairs, which can be stored flat or hung in a

cupboard, are useful for the times when extra seating is needed but should not be used for small children who can easily slip between the seat and the back. If the folding chairs are too low for your dining table, add cushions.

Storage space Remember that you are likely to need a place either in the dining room or close by to store glasses, cutlery and china. This can be a traditional sideboard (which can also be used for carving and serving food) or modern unit furniture. If there is not enough space in the dining room for storage, look for a suitable area close by and use a trolley.

△ *The right position*
This table extends with the legs at the ends where they don't impede diners.

△ *The wrong position*
The position of the legs makes this table uncomfortable when extended.

△ *The gate-leg table*
Gate-leg tables are always uncomfortable for dining.

SPACE-SAVING DINING

Build a bench Corner bench seating is a good way to create a dining area in limited space. Benches and tables are available from DIY stores. If the dining area is in the kitchen, a low

wall behind the bench makes a good divider.

Custom-built dining Another way to solve the problem of separating the dining area from the kitchen is to ask a fitted kitchen manufacturer to

design a scheme which incorporates a table and an open shelf room divider. Look through some catalogues and interior design magazines for ideas which might suit your room.

Storing
and Serving

In these often fraught times how good it is to sit down with family and friends in an atmosphere which is congenial and where the scene has been set as invitingly as possible. Whether it's the gathering together of a family to share a meal at the end of the day, or friends invited in for fine food and pleasant company, dining in an area specifically set aside for that purpose can make it a very special occasion.

However, unless a room is convenient to use, an unnecessary strain is imposed on entertaining. And for family meals it's tempting to make do with perching in the kitchen or having a quick snack in front of the television. With just a bit of extra effort, it's possible to bring your dining room into more general use: for light family meals as well as special occasions, and for breakfast as well as the evening meal.

Even if you dine close by your kitchen, ill-considered storage can lead to tedious treks to and fro. Consider having cutlery and crockery handily nearby so laying the table isn't a chore. Keeping a stack of trays exactly where they are needed can save effort. If your kitchen is more than a step away, consider letting a trolley help you to take the strain.

The pleasure of enjoying a fine meal will be diminished if there isn't enough elbow room to serve it properly. A surface for serving and holding everything that's needed as the meal proceeds – wine, salad, cheeses, fruit – will enable the hostess to relax along with the rest of the company.

Dressing up
This mellowed pine table and matching dresser are sturdily practical for family meals and also set an inviting scene for grander entertaining. The dresser provides plenty of storage exactly where it's needed: table linen in the cupboard base, and pretty china displayed in the glazed top.

SETTING THE SCENE

To get maximum everyday use from your dining room, it's necessary first to examine your customary practice to see if you can establish a smoother, speedier flow from kitchen to dining room and back. Convenient storage and ease of serving need special attention. If the dining room is some distance from the kitchen, can you store china, cutlery, glass and mats closer, ready for laying up the table? Would oven-to-tableware speed the process?

· The conventional solution to combined storage and serving is a sideboard that matches the dining-room suite. Some have a pull-out leaf for serving. Alternatively, if you hanker after a country-style dresser but haven't space for it in a small kitchen, think about siting it in your dining room.

A dresser provides closed storage, an open or glazed display section and often a surface for serving. A similar effect can be achieved with shelves, perhaps in an alcove, with a cupboard below. Open space can be used to display pretty china. Cupboards and drawers need to be arranged so that nothing gets buried: it's easy to forget about a pretty bowl or that special serving knife for fish or flans.

If your dining room is small, you may have to use the kitchen for storage, but you will still need a surface for serving, particularly for special occasions. A narrow side table would take up little space and be about the right height; or a wide, sturdy shelf on one wall could be used. Remember your serving area may need protection against heat and spillage, so keep a tray or mats handy.

If the dining room is small and the gathering large, the table might well get uncomfortably crammed. It's helpful to have a surface nearby for wine, serving dishes and sauces, salads and cheese, as well as space to stack used crockery and glasses as the meal proceeds. With forethought, the hostess won't have to be constantly on the go, fetching and carrying for each course. Even if space is limited, remember to leave a passageway around the table so access is possible and guests aren't trapped in their seats.

A well-planned trolley ready laid with essentials will speed movement between kitchen and dining room. Some trolleys have adjustable shelving to suit specific needs. And if space is tight, look for a trolley that folds flat for easy storage when it's not in use.

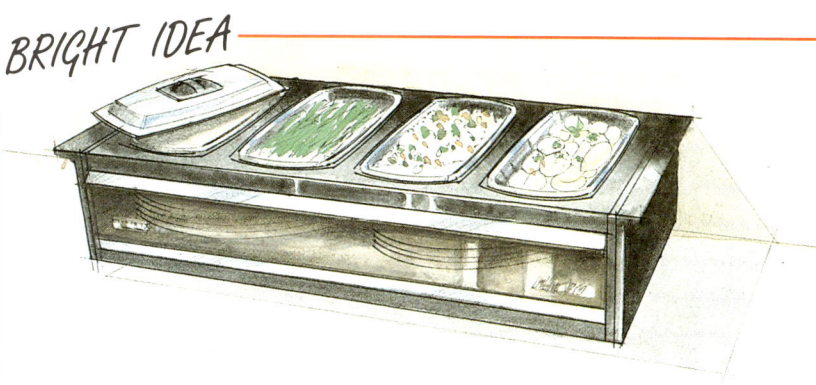

SERVING IT HOT

If you like your food piping hot, an electrically heated side server will warm the plates and keep your meal heated in covered glass dishes. It's particularly useful in a family where second helpings are popular! If you frequently cater for larger gatherings of eight people or more, heated trolleys are available, with sliding trays which can be used for carving and serving.

◁ *Dining divide*
A combined kitchen and dining room can be well served by a partial room divider like the one shown here. A divider keeps separate the different functions of the two areas, so that meals can be enjoyed away from the preparation point.

Here the base unit provides additional work surface for the kitchen area, and a convenient serving space when a meal is under way. Necessities can be put on to trays for easy transfer from kitchen to dining room.

▽ *Movable feast*
The inconvenience of a distant kitchen can be eased by wheeling in all you need on a trolley. This can also alleviate pressure on space in a small dining room. There are fold-up versions that store away neatly.

Look out for a trolley that's sturdy enough to be used for serving, too. Between courses, used dishes can be stacked ready for the return journey after the meal. Trolleys can be bought in various finishes, to suit modern or more traditional styles.

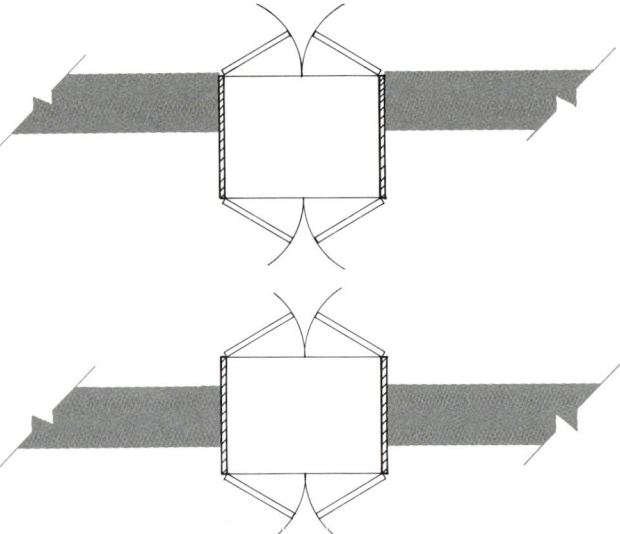

△ Pine design

A robust old pine dresser gives natural charm to a country-style dining room. Closed cupboards and drawers hold the cutlery, china and so on needed for eating, while open shelves display favourite items: this sort of dresser looks good if it's crammed full with treasures. The base is topped by a shelf wide enough for serving when a meal is under way.

▷ Double access

An alternative idea, if kitchen and dining rooms are adjacent, is to install a two-way cupboard between the rooms, with access from either side. After washing up, dishes can be stored ready for dining; meals can go straight from kitchen to dining room through a large hatch. The cupboard could be centrally positioned between rooms, or have its main bulk in either room, wherever space permits (see plan of two possible positions, left). Remember, when knocking through, a load-bearing wall must be reinforced.

◁ **Window servery**
Limited space for storage
and serving needs ingenious
solutions. Here the original
windowsill has been built out
to provide useful storage
below, and the deep sill
makes an attractive display
and serving area. Tiles are a
very practical surface for
serving as they are not
damaged by warm dishes or
spillages, but avoid letting
anything heavy drop on
them. A less robust serving
surface, such as polished
wood, will need protection,
perhaps with a plastic or
oilcloth covering and mats or
trivets.

△ **Throughway**
A view of the double-access cupboard,
pictured on the left, showing the
convenient arrangement of shelving and
good-sized serving hatch.

13

▷ **Collecting together**
Your favourite china needn't be housed in special dressers or sideboards. An inexpensive idea when you first move house is to use adjustable shelving in your dining room. Even a makeshift arrangement, carried through with confidence, can create an original display. A practical point to note is that most of the collection shown here is put to regular use, otherwise dusting could be a real trial!

▽ **Storage style**
In this traditional setting the necessities for dining can be stored conveniently close to the table. In addition, a corner cupboard displays a collection of silver, and the other furniture is robust enough to provide serving space if required.

△ **Best cellar**
There's nothing so cheerless as an unused fire; but this has been put to imaginative use as a makeshift cellar. Most wine will survive in normal dining room temperatures. Make sure it's stored on its side, well away from a radiator, and in a place where it is likely to be undisturbed until needed.

Lighting the Dining Room

The aim of dining room lighting is to create an atmosphere which is comfortable to dine in. The contrast of light and shade in a dining room should be planned as carefully as any other aspect of the room, whether it's the position and style of furniture, or the overall colour scheme.

Your choice of lighting scheme is obviously influenced by the way you use your dining room. Some are used almost exclusively for formal dinner parties, others are family dining rooms first and foremost, which are occasionally used for entertaining guests. Some must double up as work rooms or study areas.

The lighting must be sufficiently subtle and adaptable to accommodate all these uses and moods. You need to be able to see what you are eating as well as your neighbours at the table. Yet the light must not be so bright that it kills the atmosphere you are trying to create.

Before making decisions, take a tip from the professionals and try to study the lighting in other people's homes as well as in restaurants and cafés, where the lighting has almost certainly been professionally designed.

A light fitting over the dining table itself is a definite advantage. In addition, you will need to light the serving table or sideboard – and it's a good idea to create some focal points in addition to the table. Finally, of course, there must be sufficient overall lighting.

So long as these criteria are met, you are free to choose fittings that match the style of the room – ranging from elaborate and formal chandeliers to modern, streamlined lights.

Simple and effective
On bright, sunny days this dining table needs no artificial lighting. In overcast weather (and, of course, at night) a simple pendant over the table adds to the glow of the candles, and a converted oil lamp lights the dresser.

LIGHTING THE TABLE

A light fitting directly above a table enables you to see what you are eating and defines the dining area, especially in a multi-functional room.

A pendant lamp is the most common choice, partly because the fitting itself helps to define the table. Pendant lamps need to be carefully positioned above the table (see Bright Idea). Other alternatives include surface-mounted or recessed downlighters. The latter can also discreetly boost the light from a pendant fitting.

◁ *A graceful curve*
The long, flexible arm of this standard lamp reaches over the dining table and can therefore replace an ordinary pendant fitting.

▽ *Modern lights*
The tungsten halogen uplighter in the corner of this dining room bounces light off the ceiling on to the table. Candles alone therefore are sufficient to light the table itself.

△ **Twice as bright**
A long dining table is best lit by two or three pendant lamps. If the table is extendable, hang one pendant above the centre and others at each end.

◁ **Classically simple shapes**
A black lampshade to match the chairs sets the style in this dining room.

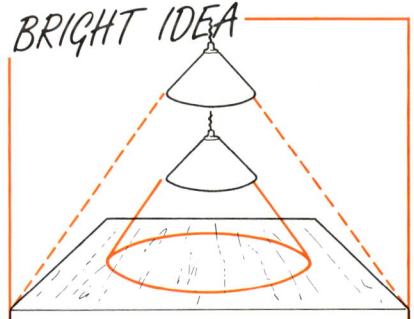

BRIGHT IDEA

Hang a pendant lamp high above a table to shed a large but relatively diffuse pool of light. For more intimate meals, a lamp nearer the table will cast a more concentrated pool of light.

△ **A variety of light sources**
The lighting of this dining room has been planned so that several sources of light are available, as the occasion demands. The wall unit, which has an integral light source to illuminate the display of china, is flanked by modern uplighters. A table lamp on the sideboard makes serving easy.

◁ **A crown-silvered bulb**
If the light bulb projects below the shade of a pendant lamp, fit a crown-silvered bulb which is decorative in itself and reduces glare by masking the filament. Used in a reflective shade, a crown-silvered bulb also produces a sharper beam of light.

△ **Side lights**
A serving table or sideboard in a dining room should be as well-lit as other work areas in the home. Downlighters positioned above the sideboard can therefore serve a dual function: they provide working light as well as highlighting the sideboard, creating a focal point in the room other than the dining table.

A row of recessed or surface-mounted downlighters can be positioned to cast separate or overlapping pools of light.

LIGHTING THE WHOLE ROOM

As well as adequate general lighting, a dining room benefits from good task lighting and one or more focal points in addition to the table itself.

Overall lighting is particularly important if a dining room is not used solely for evening entertaining. Wall lights, often hung on either side of a fireplace, are a traditional solution and are available in modern as well as classic styles, perhaps to match an elaborate chandelier over the table. Recessed or surface-mounted downlighters or a tungsten halogen uplighter are other suitable solutions.

Focal points and task lighting While the table is a natural focal point in a dining room, it's a good idea to create additional points of visual interest in the room. That way, you can highlight the table without having to dine in a single pool of light surrounded by semi-darkness.

A table or sideboard that's used for serving needs clear lighting while it's in use. If you fit a dimmer switch for this light, the lighting can be turned down when you have finished working there, or when the meal is nearing its end, to hide dirty plates and empty serving dishes.

Other focal points could include a painting, a flower arrangement, or a large and attractive ornament on a bookcase or occasional table – even architectural details such as an attractive fireplace. Use picture lights, wallwashers and spotlights to create glowing pools of light. A standard lamp adds visual interest as well as creating a focal point.

If the dining room boasts an attractive bay or bow window, consider installing strip lighting behind the pelmet to draw attention to the window and the curtains or blinds. Strip lighting hidden above a pelmet or coving will bounce light off a pale ceiling to produce a gentle glow round the room's perimeter that's ideal as background.

CANDLELIGHT

Although candles throw a romantic glow, just one or two candles on a dining table rarely cast enough light to eat by. To boost the light without sacrificing the intimate mood, either group a number of candles together or direct the beam of a downlighter on to the candles. A rise-and-fall lamp can be raised so high that you feel you are dining solely by candlelight.

△ *Dining by candlelight*
By scattering subdued lighting at various points in this dining room, sufficient light is provided without disturbing the gentle atmosphere.

▽ *A gentle glow*
For a very intimate atmosphere, the light of a single candle is boosted by a pair of wall-hung candle brackets and a lamp on the sideboard.

BRIGHT IDEA

Mirror image For a really unusual and attractive focal point on a festive occasion, mass a collection of candles in front of a mirror. The reflected flames are magnified, throwing a sparkling light.

Candles for Character

With the exception of the odd stub kept for emergencies, candles are now regarded as a luxury rather than a necessity. Yet they are the cheapest and most effective way to alter completely the character and atmosphere of a room. As they are not the most efficient source of light, it is best not to rely on them alone: use them in conjunction with back-up or background lighting.

Scented or odourlesss, coloured or white, tall or short, thin or fat, there are many different varieties of candles readily available. Candlesticks come in as many shapes and finishes, be they plain, utilitarian or highly ornate.

Coloured candles can blend in with or accent the decoration in the room, whilst arrangements of dried or fresh flowers round the base of a candle can be changed to suit the season. When used with dried flowers and other combustible materials, do make sure that the candle isn't left to burn too low.

△ *Colourful centrepiece*
Elegant table settings need not rely on the presence of expensive crystal or valuable silver candlesticks. Here, dried flowers have been arranged around the base of a fat blue candle. The flowers used are predominantly mauve and pink: notice how this theme recurs in the cloth. The folded napkins have blue ribbon 'rosebuds' in them to match the bow which has been set into the decoration at the base of the candle.

◁ *Drama of candlelight*
The incandescent glow of a single candle placed towards the centre of this table is enhanced by the strong, narrow beam of light emitted from an overhead source. The qualities of both types of light complement each other beautifully. The dramatic lighting is reflected off the polished marble table top, the facets of the cut glass candlestick and the crystal glasses.

The colours in the room and the place settings are enhanced by the orange lilies in the main flower arrangement, and the use of two smaller orangey-red blooms with the candlestick.

△ **Candle light**
A collection of candles in glass 'chimneys' are grouped in the centre of this unusual dining table. Of varying heights and proportions, they emit a good level of light, are protected from draughts and are cleverly interspersed with small floral arrangements in similar vases.

△ **Lustrous light**
This brightly decorated dining area is lit with candles, backed up by wall sconces. Four simple antique brass candlesticks combine with two brass candle lamps placed slightly in front of them. This style of lamp is more often associated with paraffin-burning lamps.

◁ **The light of luxury**
Pastel-coloured candles in crystal candelabras are co-ordinated with the table linen in this formal dining room. The same pale candles are also used in the silver candelabra on the sideboard. The combination of white china, pastel and lace table linen, cut glass and pale candles creates a light and airy atmosphere, emphasizing rather than detracting from the grandeur of the setting.

Dining in Style

The basic requirements for a dining room are a table for eating at and chairs to sit on. Although style is largely a personal matter, you'll almost certainly want something in keeping with the rest of the house. This doesn't necessarily mean being chained to a particular period: Victorian style furniture in a turn-of-the-century house, for example. Modern furniture can look good in an older setting providing there's empathy between furniture and surroundings.

Think, too, of your normal eating needs. If there are children about, you don't want to be forever anxious about delicate surfaces, so compromise with a scheme for relaxed everyday gatherings that can be smartened for guests.

Make sure the room is really comfortable and easy to manage — spend time sorting out details like easy-care surfaces and handy storage. The most elegant furniture won't hold much appeal if the lighting is gloomy or harsh:

use dimmers as part of an adjustable scheme, perhaps with rise-and-fall pendants above the table and wallwashers, picture lights or downlighters for subtle focal points elsewhere.

A fine meal is far less appetising in a room that's distinctly chilly, so good heating is important. Though there's nothing quite like a blazing coal fire, be honest: will it be lit for quick family meals or only grander occasions? Coal-effect gas may be more practical as a cheerful focal point and to provide a source of extra heat, particularly on chilly nights.

Modern lines
An unusual solid beech underframe and curved chairs give distinction to this suite. It's a classic style that isn't likely to date, and would sit nicely in a modern or traditional setting. In this room the soft creamy backdrop is kept deliberately sparse.

TRADITIONAL STYLE

Few of us are in a position to collect together a Regency table and six or eight matching chairs. It is, though, possible to give a traditional feel to a room without spending a fortune.

Borrow library books on traditional interiors to catch the essence of an era: adapt ideas as faithfully or freely as you please. Edwardian copies of antique furniture are less pricey and can have a fine patina. Alternatively, some modern reproduction furniture is very good indeed: the best isn't cheap but usually has the advantage of being easier to care for than the real thing.

If you're working to a budget but are determined to have authentic pieces, scour junk shops and auction rooms for interesting old chairs that are superficially dilapidated but structurally sound; if they have a similar feel they don't need to match exactly. Improvise by draping a big cloth over a round chipboard table, with a lace overcloth for entertaining. For everyday use some firms will coat a favourite fabric in plastic for wipe-clean convenience.

For a country air there's still a lot of old pine about – dressers and side cupboards as well as tables and chairs. Modern well-seasoned pine with a distressed finish looks convincingly aged.

Let wallcoverings follow the style – anything from a Regency stripe to whitewashed simplicity. Paint effects like marbling or ragging could work well. And catch the appropriate mood at the windows: fringes and frills, flouncing drapes with cord tiebacks, pretty lace or café half-curtains.

Often it's little details that give the flavour of a period. Search around for extras to give a cumulative effect: an antique or modern butler's tray, wall sconces, a good mirror over the mantel, candles, old brass fixtures, polished glass decanters, even a luxuriant aspidistra in the corner to produce a distinctly Victorian spirit.

◁ *Traditional taste*
A gradual accumulation of just the right accessories gives a definite identity to a room. Handsome old furniture in this room is enhanced by a fine service and well-chosen accessories: touches of brass and polished glass about the room combine for a warm gleam. Most of the ornaments are placed fairly low to be appreciated by diners. Some accessories can be rotated from time to time so they don't grow stale!

A dado-level border is cleverly diverted to frame the window, and the translucent blind is a good idea as it shields a glaring sun and gives privacy while still admitting natural light into the room.

▷ *Dining comfort*
Fully upholstered chairs are ideal for lingering over a meal: for a practical finish treat fabric with stain-resistant spray. Curved arms allow the carvers to be drawn up comfortably to the table. An appropriate backdrop is provided by painted dado and cornice teamed with traditional wallpaper.

◁ **New into old**

A kitchen connection need not prevent you having a traditional dining room, if that's what you want. This interior has been given a period feel, and the dining room reflects that old-fashioned charm though the oak gate-leg table and chairs in 18th-century style are in fact modern, and built to withstand the rigours of everyday use.

From the contemporary wooden blinds to the mirror with candle sconces – a genuine old piece – this room is an admirable mix of old and new. For example, you can see how the lighting combines traditional grace with modern practicality. Once the company is assembled the functional kitchen lights can be switched off and recessed downlighters dimmed so that the meal is enjoyed in candlelight.

MODERN MOOD

Though there's adventurous new dining furniture about, a modern suite doesn't necessarily involve a break with tradition. If you don't want to play conventionally safe, investigate the latest Italian designs – very cool, very chic – but take care that you don't end up with a style you'll tire of or something that soon dates.

For sleek city living, look for stained black tables and leather and chrome chairs. Modern classics, such as the cantilevered Bauhaus chair, fit in well with this sophisticated elegance. If black is too sombre, build up the style with sleek light-wood furniture.

The coolly modern city look is nowhere near as spare as would satisfy a minimalist. For this, nothing must distract from the simplicity of pure line. Root out anything that's even a touch sentimental or romantic. Store everything but the barest of essentials well out of sight. Unless you're an out-and-out purist you may find an empty void too stark. A little skilful compromise is quite in order – perhaps a big pot with dried seedheads, or a well-lit wallhanging. Once you get a feel for a style you'll soon gain enough confidence to be able to discriminate between appropriate and jarring elements.

Have a neutral ground for your modern dining room, with clear accent colours used sparingly and plain roman or venetian blinds at the window. Hang large abstract prints on the wall, look for concealed lighting or leggy Italian lights. Choose plants or flowers with a strong architectural quality rather than softening foliage.

◁ *Material mix*
A combination of marble table with leather and chrome cantilevered chairs makes a dramatic dining centrepiece: on this sort of scale, and with such splendid materials, little else is needed in the room. A plain rug helps define the dining area, and is sensibly big so that chairs can be drawn in and out without difficulty.

If you like a spare, disciplined approach look for basics in first-rate materials with simple but satisfying lines. Limit accessories to a well-considered minimum. Proper organization of storage is essential so all that precious emptiness doesn't attract clutter.

LIGHT STYLE

For a modern chandelier effect, hang several lights above a dining table. Mix the colours to suit your room scheme and experiment with lights suspended at slightly different heights. A separate dimmer switch for each light would allow a great variety of mood.

If you want to use curly cable – and it does look attractive – let thin wire take the weight of the lights so the cable stays curled.

▽ Dining space

Chrome on table and chairs adds a gleam to the starkness of black in a grouping that has an almost Japanese purity. Venetian blinds give a muted light to augment the general calm. It's all offset by an elegant beech floor.

Once the basics are established, attend to those details that give an uplift. Here, the severity is softened by coral table dressings, including fan-fold napkins that introduce just the right degree of shape and light relief to the table.

△ Contemporary classic

Good modern furniture fits in well with a variety of settings. Here, hand-built pieces look comfortably at home in an old country rectory though they could equally well grace a modern scheme. There's no absence of sunlight in this dining corner, but light wood is a particularly good choice in a room that's inclined to be dark.

All the pieces in this range – display cabinet, table and seating – are in solid ash with distinctive rounded detailing. Different types of seats – side and carver chairs and a cane-backed banquette – provide interesting variation in shape.

Some of the finest new furniture around today is inspired by the best traditions of the past but nevertheless retains a distinctly modern quality. First-rate materials are combined with strong, pleasing lines to produce good-natured furniture that will stand the test of time.

◁ Dining den

Not everyone has a separate – or even a large – dining area. Here, the awkwardly narrow shape has been turned to advantage. Red gloss is a bold choice for a small space, but it gives friendly warmth to this area, and the built-in sofa, upholstered to match the chairs, is nicely plump and inviting.

This sort of fine old table seems to demand the special magic of candles, which can be boosted with other lighting that's versatile enough to meet different needs. The whole area looks just the place for guests to linger over coffee at the end of a meal.

▷ Table arrangements

In many flats and conversions space is at a premium, and ingenuity and an open-minded approach to planning are called for. A dining table doesn't have to be placed right in the middle of the room; in fact an alternative arrangement, perhaps ranged along or butting up to a wall, is often more intimate for dining and won't obtrude at other times.

If the room is used for other purposes, the table can be a display area for collections like these ducks and a grand old pot. The very modern strip light is a good surprise element in a featureless corner.

Dining Rooms for Entertaining

An outside view is unimportant for evening entertaining, but for day-time use, a dining room that leads on to the garden is particularly pleasant. An adjoining patio or balcony is the perfect spot for aperitifs or coffee in summer.

The dimensions are also important, as a minimum of 12-16 square metres is usually required to accommodate six people comfortably around a table with enough room for them to get in and out. But even a dining room which is too small to house storage units or a sideboard as well as the dining table and chairs is an improvement over the living/dining room or kitchen/diner arrangement as all the preparation and clearing away can be done out of sight of the guests.

Patterned co-ordination
Strongly patterned wallpaper and curtain fabric – which might seem overdone elsewhere in the home – form the basis of the decor of this dining room. The off-white, pinky-red and green are echoed in furniture, crockery, tablecloth and cushions.

A dining room used for the sole purpose of entertaining is one of those rare rooms where you have extensive freedom of choice in both design and planning. Used for only a few hours at a time, and mostly during the evening, this is one area where you can exercise the creative rather than the down-to-earth side of your decorating skills.

Wall- and floorcoverings, furniture, furnishings and lighting can all be chosen largely on aesthetic grounds, for their ability to create mood and atmosphere rather than to withstand the rough-and-tumble of family life.

Of course, you cannot totally ignore the practical aspects of a room in which food is served, but you can afford to experiment with some more dramatic schemes which maybe you would not contemplate trying out in regularly-used family rooms.

Siting the room Ideally, the dining room should be close to the kitchen, with an interconnecting door or serving hatch. In practice, though, your choice is likely to be influenced by the position and functions of other rooms.

GETTING THE STYLE RIGHT

Within reason, there's no need to curb your imagination when decorating the dining room. The colours and patterns can be bold and dramatic – chosen to enhance the sense of occasion rather than to relax.

The style depends on the type of entertaining you prefer. A room used mainly for having supper with close friends may well be entirely different from one in which formal dinner parties or business suppers are to be held. The two need not be mutually exclusive, though. With creative planning, it is possible to incorporate both styles in the same room – it is surprising what a switch of tableware and linen and different lighting can achieve.

Lighting Good lights enhance a well-laid table, highlight and compliment the food and help create an atmosphere that makes people feel at ease.

For the best effect, a combination of

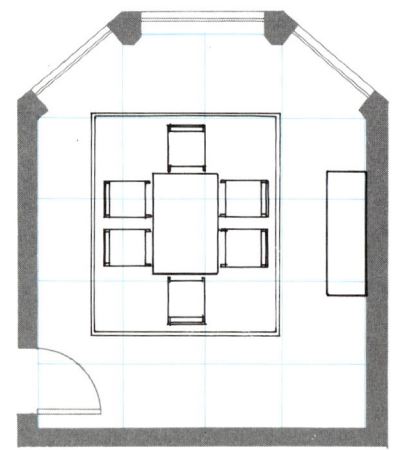

Scale: 1 square = 1 metre square

◁ *Up to date*
Traditional bay windows and wooden flooring blend well with smart, modern furniture and furnishings.

▽ *Formal elegance*
Rich shades of gold, luxurious velvet fabrics and a polished parquet floor make this dining room perfect for formal dinner parties.

light fittings is the answer. It's unwise to rely on a single ceiling fitting which tends to restrict your flexibility. Similarly, wall-lights, or floor lamps standing in the corner of the room, should not be used as the sole source of light as they cast a shadow over both the guests and their meal.

So you'll need some sort of lighting immediately above the table. The table light must enable diners to see what they are eating without subjecting them to a harsh glare. A rise-and-fall fitting above the table is an excellent choice – but do not place it so low down that it obstructs the guests' view of each other.

A dimmer switch allows you to adjust lighting levels to create the right mood for the occasion.

Away from the table, the illumination of the serving area should be slightly stronger and can be provided by a standard or table lamp, or spotlights mounted on the wall above.

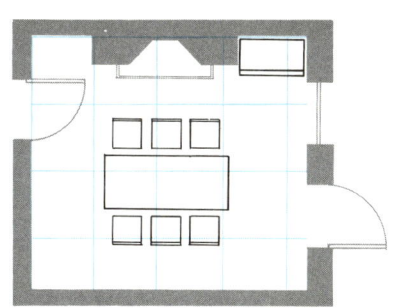

Scale: 1 square = 1 metre square

△ **A friendly atmosphere**
Informality is the keynote to this farmhouse-style dining room, ideal for family get-togethers. The pine table in the centre of the room allows easy access all round and a glass-fronted dresser combines storage and display.

◁ *Country classic*
A change of wall treatment, lighting and floorcovering, and the addition of co-ordinating curtains and a set of matching chairs, give the room above a more sophisticated yet still casual feel.

CHOOSING DINING FURNITURE

Although a dining suite placed centrally in a room may seem to have a generous amount of space around it when not in use, it's important to think about the comfort and safety of both diners and host when the room is actually in use. In terms of space, you should allow about 60cm for each diner and chair, and a minimum of another 45cm for the diner to push the chair back, or for the host to pass behind with a serving dish. A dado rail at chair-back height helps to protect precious wallpaper from being damaged by careless guests.

The dining table When buying a new or secondhand table, bear in mind that a full place setting is between 60 and 70cm long, so a minimum size for six diners is about 150cm long for a rectangular table and 120cm in diameter for a round one.

In a small room, a round table accommodates more people comfort-ably than a rectangular one and, with no one at the 'head', tends to suit informal occasions. If space is tight, an extendable table might be a better choice, to seat four in comfort and stretch out to six or eight by means of a drop-in or pull-out leaf. In a generously-proportioned rectangular dining room, a large rectangular or oval table is the obvious choice.

Dining chairs need not match each other, or indeed the table, but they must be comfortable, especially if you like guests to linger over coffee after a meal. Good back support and cush-ioned seats are desirable, and arms add additional comfort but take up more space. Allow at least 25cm of knee-room between the table and chair.

Serving tables Whether you prefer to serve guests, or let them help them-selves, you need a small table on which to put serving dishes, carve meat, set out coffee cups and so on. A narrow table with a drawer for place mats,

△ **Glowing red**
A dramatic colour scheme, with spotlights focusing attention on the painting, overcomes the uninteresting shape of this box-like room. The large expanse of strong colour combined with the bold painting might seem overpowering in, for example, a living room, but here they help to create an exciting atmosphere for dinner parties.

A fairly small round table which has an additional drop-in leaf can be extended for larger parties.

napkins and so on is ideal. A stable trolley or a shelf at a comfortable height for working on positioned in an alcove or beneath a serving hatch also does the job just as well.

For dining room storage, a traditional sideboard or a modern wall unit is a practical choice and can also sometimes double up as a serving table, providing its height suits the host.

BRIGHT IDEA

Lighting trick Dining just by candlelight is rarely a good idea unless you are having an intimate dinner for two. It is difficult to carry on a conversation, or see what one is eating, in such dim light. But candles do throw an inviting glow, and it is a good idea to supplement the light by directing the beam of a downlighter on to the candles.

▷ *Simplicity*
Dining room furniture need not necessarily be bought as a matching set. Here a heavy pine table is quite at home with lightweight bentwood chairs.

▽ *The modern touch*
High-tech furniture complements the painted brick walls of this dining room. The doors on to the patio make this an ideal spot for summer-time gatherings.

▷ A traditional feel

The architectural detail of this dining room – the shutters, cornice and fireplace – is complemented by carefully chosen fabrics, furniture and tableware.

For less formal occasions, the lace tablecloth, fine china dinner service and crystal glassware can be replaced by a simple printed cloth and, perhaps, the everyday crockery. The choice of wallpaper lends itself to both formal and informal gatherings, and the blue carpet helps to disguise stains.

▽ Practical and pretty

Natural materials combine with an abundance of greenery to create a fresh, inviting atmosphere in this dining room. The table could easily be dressed up with a floor-length tablecloth and tableware to match, or 'dressed down' with simple place mats instead of the tablecloth.

By locating the dining room next to the kitchen, the cook can serve piping hot food with a minimum of delay. If necessary, the pine dresser can double as a serving table.

Dining Areas in Living Rooms

The most used room in the house – the living/dining room – should be designed for comfort and convenience. This is where you spend time sitting, relaxing or watching TV, and where you eat evening meals and entertain.

Depending on the shape of the room and how it is decorated and furnished, it can be treated as a single room where the living and dining areas are integrated, or planned so that the two areas are separate.

Dividing the two areas The room may be divided physically by a change in shape, floor level or by an archway. Lighting can be used to change the emphasis in the two areas, or you can create the same effect with decoration, using different paint, wallpaper and floor coverings to make a definite boundary.

Another way to divide the room is with furniture, perhaps with a series of low-level cupboards that open out into the dining area or with a sofa facing towards the living room area.

Unifying the room The alternative approach is to treat the room as a single entity. Use the same decorative finishes throughout, linking the two sections with details such as a wallpaper border, or using the same fabric for the main curtains and the tablecloth. The dining area will also look less separate if you choose dining chairs that can be used for extra seating in the living room area.

LIVING/DINING ROOM LAYOUT

Where you locate each area depends largely on the shape of the room. There may be an alcove, a narrow end, or the short leg of an L-shape that is ideal for a table and chairs. Otherwise the obvious place is close to the kitchen. Modern houses are often designed with the eating area as an integral part of the living room. In older houses, the wall between the living and dining rooms may be opened up to give more space with the dining area at one end.

Versatile living
This good-looking practical space serves as a living/dining room and incorporates a study area too. The sofa, facing into the living area, creates a natural division and is backed by a console table conveniently placed for serving. Notice how the black and white floor changes level, emphasizing the difference between living and dining areas.

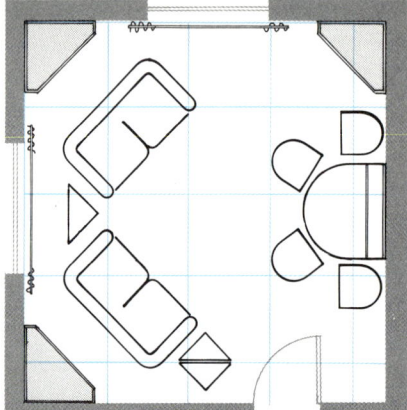

STORAGE SENSE

Any dining area needs to have enough storage space to house your china, glass, table linen and cutlery.

Old-fashioned sideboards are very useful in living/dining rooms, being slightly higher than their modern equivalents, which has a dual advantage: they are the perfect height for carving and serving food from as well as providing more storage space.

Low-level cupboards can be used for storage and as room dividers, while tall cupboards, possibly glass-fronted, make the best use of floor space.

LIGHTING

A lot of activities other than sitting and eating take place in a living/dining room, so it needs flexible lighting.

It is important to work out exactly what you use the room for and how much time you spend doing what. Identify what you do where as well as what sort of moods you want to create.

Task lighting for reading and to illuminate areas such as the stereo and the TV are a good idea, and so is a dimmer switch. You need good lighting over the table so you can see what you're eating but at the same time, the light should be subtle and flattering to faces and food. Avoid non-adjustable overhead fittings which may be in the wrong place if you decide to move the furniture around. Table or floor lamps close by give a softer glow and can also serve as task lights when the table is used for other activities.

△ Corner wise

The three corner cabinets have a surprising amount of storage space.

During meals, the sofas can be moved back and the table opened out into the room, (see plan, below). When not in use, the drop-leaf table is pushed against the wall and the dining chairs are turned round, (see plan, left).

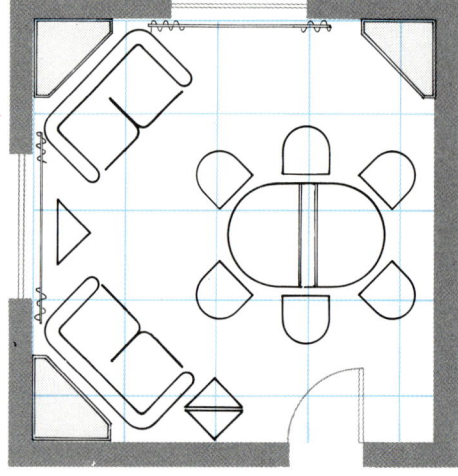

scale: 1 square = 1 metre

A flexible lighting scheme should include an adjustable light for the dining table, such as a rise-and-fall pendant or wall lights controlled by a dimmer switch, and some general light with plenty of power points for task lighting and table lamps in the living area.

wall light

rise-and-fall

uplighter

table lamp

▽ *Folding solution*

Here, instead of the drop-leaf, a long modern table which folds in half lengthways has been chosen.

As shown in the diagram right, it opens out into a full-size dining table and when folded, it makes a handsome console table, pushed back against the wall. An elegant dining chair fits neatly at either end and additional seats can be carried in from other rooms when needed.

SOFAS AND CHAIRS

As the living/dining room is used for more than one purpose, versatility should be a priority. Space may be tight, so choose chairs and sofas that aren't too bulky. If the living room furniture has to be pushed back to make room for the dining table when it is extended, make sure everything is fitted with castors or is light enough to be carried.

TABLES

Rectangular or oval tables that can be made longer or smaller are perfect for dual-purpose rooms, provided there is somewhere to store a detachable leaf when it is not required. If you don't have the room, choose a drop-leaf table, or one where the leaves are attached at either end and can be pushed into the body of the table to reduce its size.

The dining table is likely to become a social centre for a wide range of activities – conversation, homework, games and hobbies as well as mealtime get-togethers – so the table has to survive everyday wear and tear and still look its best when you are entertaining.

A table top that is durable is the most practical choice. Laminated plastic immediately comes to mind – it is tough and easy to keep clean, and although somewhat utilitarian in appearance, can be dressed up for formal occasions. Natural wood, such as oak, beech or pine, looks good and can be treated with a polyurethane seal to give a

hardwearing, natural-looking finish.

A glass topped or polished wooden table needs to be safeguarded from heat, spills and scratches with a thick tablecloth. If the tabletop is particularly good, use a felt undercloth for extra protection.

Entertaining As soon as your guests arrive and see the dining table laid for a meal it becomes the centre of attention, so it is worth dressing it up for special occasions. Even the shabbiest old table – a junk shop find, a garden or pasting table, or an old flush door supported by a pair of decorators' trestles – can be transformed with a smart linen tablecloth and a pair of candlesticks.

CHAIRS

Dining chairs don't have to match as long as there are some common visual elements such as colour, shape, upholstery and so on. Conventional chairs, tucked in position around a dining table which is not being used, can look very formal. Instead, choose chairs that can do double duty – as extra seating in the living area, kitchen or bedrooms. Chairs that stack or fold flat, canvas director's chairs and even stools are also ideal.

Comfort and practicality are as important as appearance when choosing chairs. With a permanent dining area, fixed banquette seating either side of the table makes good use of space but it can be a rather uncomfortable arrangement. Compromise with a bench on one side, and chairs opposite.

▷ *Simple colour scheme*
Storage plays a large part in the success of this living/dining room. The storage unit has cupboards and drawers for china, cutlery and tablecloths, with open shelves and illuminated glazed cupboard sections for displaying treasured possessions.

Sleek, matching chrome furniture, upholstered in pale grey against a background of peach carpets and walls, gives a feeling of space.

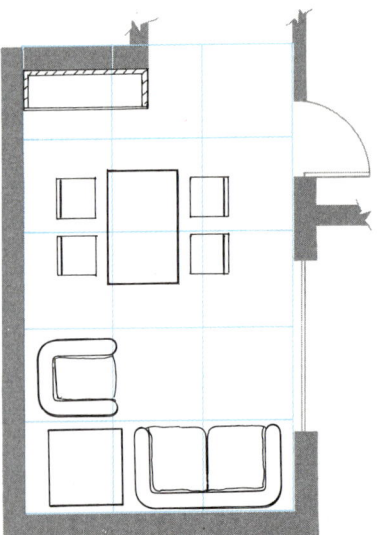

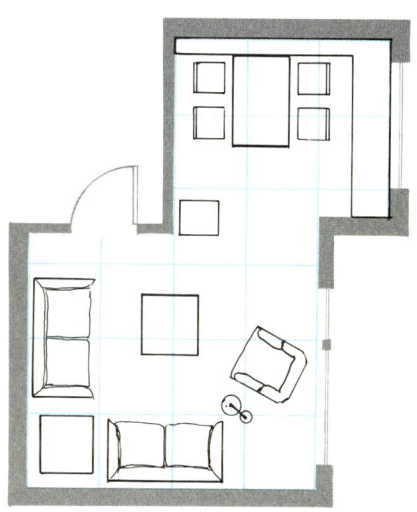

◁ **Through room**
This airy living room was designed with a dining alcove off the main seating area. The two zones are clearly defined by the change in shape but are held together, visually, by the use of the same curtain treatment and carpet.

During meals, the desk under the window becomes an extra surface for serving food and the rise-and-fall light can be lowered over the dining table.

BRIGHT IDEA

A folding screen forms a light and adjustable divider between the seating and dining area in a small living room. This makes the dining area cosier while you are eating and hides a messy table when you are relaxing after the meal.

This openwork screen divides the room without cutting out the light. Its pale colour goes well with the stripped and sealed wooden floor and simple beech dining table and bentwood chairs.

Painted antique screens can often be found in secondhand shops, or you could make your own: construct two or three rectangular wooden frames, hinge them together and drape with fabric to match your curtains or upholstery.

△ Old and new

The ground floor of this house has been knocked through to make one large living space.

The pretty round dining table is covered with a PVC cloth to protect it from scratches and spills during meals. Modern director's chairs can be used round the table or moved through into the living area for extra seating. The cheerful matching rugs provide warmth and decorative interest.

▷ Serving hatch

Easy access to the kitchen is necessary for serving food and clearing away dishes.

This extra wide serving hatch is open and provides a permanent link between the kitchen and dining area, allowing the cook to be included in conversation. The bright red pans and kitchen accessories match the lampshade, emphasizing the connection between the two areas.

Entertaining in the Living Room

The living room needs to be one of the most flexible areas of a home. It must be comfortable enough for the family to sit down together and relax in at the end of the day. But it's also the room that's used when you have guests, so it should look specially good when occasion demands.

At the planning stage, consider having two layouts, one for everyday and one for entertaining. When initially furnishing the room, you can take into account the main type of entertaining you are likely to do. Social events can usually be divided into four situations:

Family gatherings, such as at Christmas and for anniversaries. These may include making provision for small children, like putting precious ornaments beyond reach. Perhaps it would be thoughtful to supply a comfortable chair for an elderly relative to get into and out of easily.

Informal gatherings of friends for an evening. The traditional layout around the fire is unlikely to accommodate more than six guests, so consider providing two or three focal points around which seating can be grouped.

Larger parties may require space cleared for standing room, but highlight ornaments in wall units or pictures so the room doesn't look bleak. Extra surfaces for drinks could be provided by clearing bookshelves.

Formal occasions such as dinner parties may involve living room use for drinks before or after the meal. Fold-up or director's chairs could be brought in from other areas. A side table for pouring drinks would be useful.

Glowing welcome

There's nothing so welcoming as a live fire: together with warm, rich colours, it makes an inviting picture. There's a good-sized table for food and drink just a stretch away from the seating. A practical point is that the patterned carpet and soft furnishings won't show every crumb that falls. When guests are due, lamps and candles can be lit and extra chairs drawn up.

SITTING COMFORTABLY

A little forethought and some readjustment of your normal seating arrangement can make a great deal of difference to a congenial atmosphere. An evening is unlikely to go with a swing if your guests are jammed into a meanly-proportioned settee, or if chair positioning subtly excludes some of the company from full participation.

Seating combination should be decided from the outset, to serve first family requirements and be flexible enough for entertaining. Guests need to be close enough to make pleasant social contact without being squashed: seating that's too close, or too distant, will impose a strain on congeniality.

Positioning is important. Guests need not face each other directly. Settees and chairs placed at right angles may be more convivial than a face-to-face encounter over the canapes. Whatever your arrangement, try to leave a passage clear so a social group isn't disturbed by people coming and going.

Large gatherings need special provision: possibly you could arrange seating in the living room, but have ready another room for serving drinks and food, or use a dining table if you have a combined living/dining room. If you are bringing in chairs from other quarters, try to find seats of similar height. Make sure no one is left perched high and dry on the edge of the party.

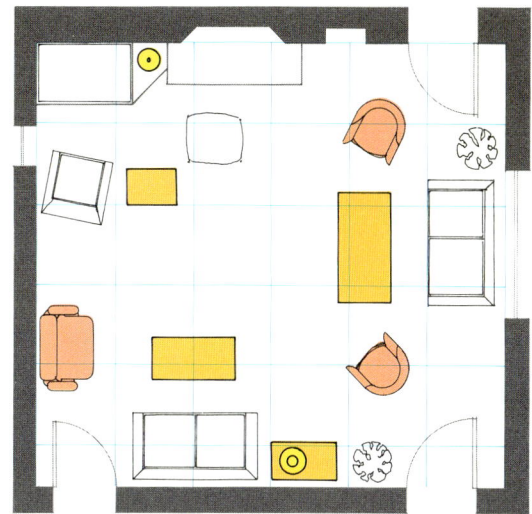

◁ ▷ *Gathering point*
Space to spread is a great benefit when the company is large, but take care to arrange seating and lights to allow guests to collect together into pleasant conversation groups. The plan on the right shows possible positioning of extra chairs (coloured pink) and a rearrangement of tables (beige) and lighting (yellow).

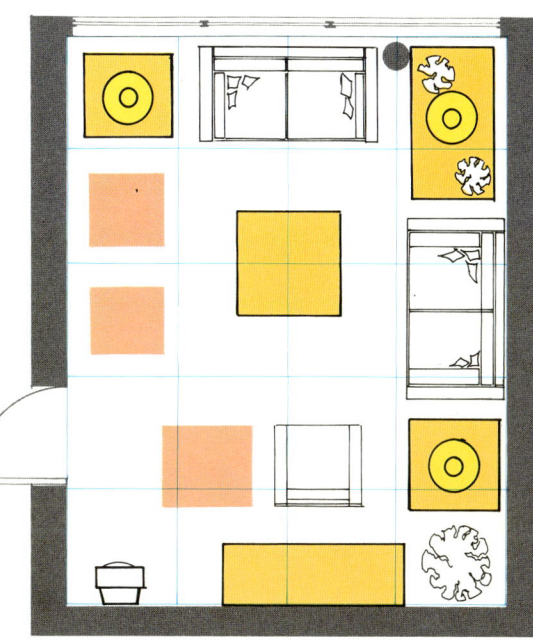

▽ ▷ *Coolly inviting*
A modern room that would lend itself well to a social gathering. Tables are handily placed for setting down drinks, and have wipe-clean surfaces which won't be damaged by spillage. On the right the plan suggests a layout for a larger group. Additional seating is shown in pink, tables are beige and lighting is coloured yellow.

Scale: 1 square = 1 metre square

◁ **On the move**
If you don't have a convenient table or other surface for drinks and glasses, a trolley may be a useful investment. It can also be used to transport party fare to and from the kitchen. One with adjustable shelving will prove the most versatile; if you don't want to use it at other times, look for a version that folds flat for storing. There are both traditional and modern styles of trolley on the market.

△ ▷ Party manoeuvres

The arrangement above would be fine for a gathering of six people, but some adjustment is needed for a larger group. As the alternative in the picture and plan shows, additional seating by the window can be included in the social circle, with a table added or shelf cleared for drinks.

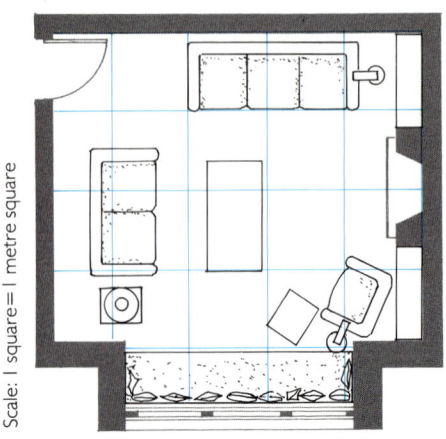

Scale: 1 square = 1 metre square

BRIGHT IDEA

Sparkling fresh These candles not only cast an attractive glow over a corner of the room, but they provide a tactful solution to a possible nuisance. There's nothing worse than a room full of stale smoke. The candle wax has been specially treated to give off a scent that will help disguise the smell of tobacco smoke. The atmosphere in a crowded room can easily become thick. A slightly-open window will allow air to circulate, but make sure no-one is in a draught.

IN THE MOOD

Lighting needs to be as versatile as possible and is an essential aspect of setting an inviting scene. The effect will of course vary according to the nature of the gathering. On a fine summer's evening you will have the benefit of natural light; guests may even want to spill out on to the patio.

Generally, lighting for entertainment should be cosily intimate – a dimmer switch is ideal, with a flexible system of freestanding table and standard lamps. You may want to cast more light on your store of drinks or music centre. Make sure that no light glares in a guest's eyes, and avoid the danger of trailing flex in a crowded room. The unused edges of a room shouldn't be left unlit; you could gently highlight special features, like a painting.

A fire will add a lovely glow to the room, and softly-flickering candles can brighten a dark corner. Sweet-smelling candles are available, and those that freshen smoke-thick air. Take care when there are many guests about – fit a guard to keep party frocks well away from a fire, and site candles safely.

Music speakers should be positioned away from a seating group, preferably at high level. If you want to put them directly on a hard surface such as wood, use an insulating mat or small carpet sample to deaden reverberation. The deck will need to be sited for easy operation, but keep it well away from a surface used for drinks to avoid accidental damage.

△ *Dancing light*
Candles have their own special magic which can transform even an ordinary room into a marvellous setting for a social occasion. Group different heights together for added sparkle.

◁ *Conversation piece*
A pleasant setting for six, which can easily be enlarged to contain a sizeable gathering. A nest of tables could provide versatile surfaces for drinks.

SET-DOWN POINTS

Guests don't want to sit with a glass (and perhaps a plate) in hand all evening. Having no convenient surface to offload on to except the floor is awkward and risky, particularly in a crowded room. If the seating is to be arranged around a central occasional table, can everyone reach?

Tables for setting down drinks can be brought from other areas, and placed at strategic points. A nest of tables would lend itself to flexible arrangement. For a large makeshift surface for drinks, you could place a long piece of chipboard between two small square tables, and cover it all with a nice cloth. You could also clear a temporary space on a bookshelf or wall unit that's within arm's reach.

Remember to protect any polished surfaces with mats, coasters, or a sheet of attractive PVC.

Trays and trolleys are a great asset when you are entertaining. Large trays placed on occasional tables will protect a delicate surface from spills, and they can be carried straight out to the kitchen at the end of the evening. A trolley can be used as a set-down point for food and drink. It can also transport party fare from the kitchen and remove all the used glasses and general debris when guests depart at the end of the evening.

◁ *Swinging spirits*
It's good to have your stock of drinks readily available for entertaining, but you may not want them displayed at other times. This concealed drinks cabinet swings away when the party is over. Whether you keep your drinks in an open or closed unit, if you have an extensive range try to provide storage space that allows room for the pouring and mixing of drinks.

▽ *Entertaining style*
An elegant room that has everything on hand for a special occasion. Drinks and glasses are housed in the wall unit, and a nest of tables can be drawn out and placed conveniently close to the seating arrangement.

Dining in the Kitchen

By its very nature, dinner is a formal meal, traditionally enjoyed in the dining room. This is all very well if your home is relatively large and follows a conventional, formal layout, but in many homes today, a completely separate dining room is a luxury which cannot be accommodated.

Yet the concept of 'dining' – as opposed to just 'eating' – is important to almost every family at some time or other. Planning for formal meals is even more important for those without a dining room than for families which can

easily seat twenty for dinner. In a combined living/dining room, well-chosen furniture and the use of room dividers can create the effect of a separate room, if desired.

Creating a formal atmosphere with only the kitchen available poses a greater challenge. The basic decision is to define exactly what one means by 'formal'. It could be that 'dining' simply involves a family meal of several courses, as opposed to everyone eating quickly on the run. Or 'dining' may mean sitting down at the kitchen table

with friends to enjoy a leisurely meal that is carefully prepared and presented, but where the day-to-day kitchen atmosphere is perfectly acceptable. Finally, the kitchen may have to play host to a really formal dinner party, complete with the 'best' crockery, silver and napery.

So long as the kitchen is large enough to hold a table and several chairs, almost any style can be accommodated. All that needs to be decided is what style will predominate. Your preferences will, naturally, dictate the choice of kitchen units and furniture, the colour scheme, lighting and other essential items.

Practical and formal
Simplicity is the keynote of this kitchen/dining room. Identical materials and a simple colour scheme give continuity of style, while the lighting helps to differentiate the two functions of the room. The U shape hides the kitchen area from view, and a ducted air vent takes care of unwanted steam and cooking smells.

BRIGHT IDEA

PLANNING A KITCHEN/DINER
A major consideration in the planning of kitchen/dining rooms is the fact that almost everything the cook does cannot be hidden from the guests.

While only a separate dining room can remove these problems entirely, they can be minimized by a room divider – or even turned to advantage as the guests share the cook's 'performance'! As in any performance, the keys to success are preparation and good props.

Minimize the work to be done after the guests arrive by choosing a menu which demands little last-minute preparation. (A cooker hood removes the traces of earlier cooking.) Pots and pans should be pretty as well as practical, and oven-to-tableware eliminates the need for separate serving dishes: Keep pre-cooked food warm on a hotplate.

▽ *Dividing the space*
This home adopts an unusual method of separating cooking and dining areas. The cooker and storage space have been incorporated into a partition which effectively blocks off working space from the dining area. A cooker hood eliminates cooking smells, and the work surface doubles as a serving hatch.

A flexible divider Hang curtains between the cooking and dining areas of a kitchen/dining room to give a simple and flexible divider.

The curtains make a relatively inexpensive room divider – they can be drawn closed for an intimate dinner party or while a meal is in progress, or left open on casual occasions. Since both sides are open to view, budget for enough fabric to make 'double-sided' curtains.

Hiding the debris Nothing spoils the effect of a dinner party more than piles of dirty dishes. A deep, double sink into which dishes may be stacked (or better still a dishwasher), allows the debris of each course to be cleared away in a matter of moments. Try to have most of the saucepans and preparation dishes cleared away before the meal starts.

Keep the cooking and dining areas as separate as possible. If space is limited, consider a drop-leaf or gateleg table and folding chairs that can be stacked neatly away to ease everyday space restrictions.

▽ *Dining room elegance*
Here the inevitable kitchen clutter is elegantly housed in solid wood units which are sophisticated enough to grace the most traditional of dining room schemes. The overall impression is of a separate dining room where guests can enjoy a formal dinner party in a setting which skilfully excludes any hint of the adjoining work area.

△ *Prettily pastel*
In this light-coloured scheme the same setting is given a more gentle, relaxed treatment than the formal elegance pictured at left. Unobtrusive concealed lighting can be brought into variable play, and pastel colours combined with careful placing of flowers and plants give a cosy, almost cottage-like feel to a dining area where friends can relax over a shared meal tucked away from the business end of the room.

THE RIGHT ATMOSPHERE

In a kitchen/dining room, it is important to pay particular attention to the style of both the cooking and the dining areas. Start by making a careful choice of kitchen units and worktops – styles vary from ultra-modern to very traditional units.

The chosen finish can be carried through to the dining table and chairs. Alternatively, a complete contrast can be created between the food preparation and dining areas.

The formal effect can be heightened by selecting elegant crockery, cutlery and table linen as well as accessories such as candlesticks and place mats.

The work area need not appear totally functional during dinner parties. Strategically placed decorative items, perhaps as simple as plants or flowers, will soften utilitarian surfaces.

Colour planning plays it role too. Light, airy colours may be chosen for the work areas of the kitchen, with more formal tones used in the dining area.

The finishing touch can often be provided by effective lighting. Try to arrange the circuits so that the food preparation and dining areas can be switched independently. In this way, light in the work area can be reduced once the meal is served, focusing attention on the dining area. This, too, can benefit from a dimmer switch to create exactly the right mood.

△ *Suspended divider*

In this combined scheme concealed lighting in the kitchen area provides workmanlike and stylish illumination while the more romantic candelabra-style lighting is reserved for the dining area. Suspended copper cookware above an island unit and the elaborate candelabra break up the regularity of the scheme. The polished wooden floor and warm-toned units blend to add welcoming warmth.

◁ **Light contrast**

With the same arrangement of units, but a change of colour scheme, dining furniture and lighting, this kitchen is given a more sophisticated, modern feel.

The adaptable modern lighting can emphasize the dining area once the guests are seated. Dimmer switches could be used to provide bright illumination or more subtle variations of mood. A tiled floor and splashes of yellow link the adjoining areas, making the overall effect stylish but not severe.

▽ **Cool combination**

Space may be limited in this crisply modern room but light colours, clean lines and a minimum of fuss create a mood of inviting coolness. Once the main features have established the basic scheme, you can experiment by adding touches of vibrant colour and plants to enliven and soften the effect.

▷ Conservatory style

Lack of space is one of the main problems encountered when it is necessary to dine in the kitchen. If a kitchen/dining room is not large, one solution is to move the entire room into an extension. Here, a large conservatory-style extension creates a spacious environment for both dining and cooking. Large glazed panels let in masses of daylight to provide a light and airy atmosphere.

▽ Adding on

By moving the kitchen into a ground floor extension, sufficient space has been created for comfortable dining and cooking. An open doorway links the dining and cooking areas, while plain white walls and the use of wood for the furniture and the kitchen worktop provide visual links.

Dining Rooms for Young Families

Unless you have the luxury of lots of space, it is unlikely that a dining room can be given over exclusively to eating. With children, it probably has many purposes in addition to family meals and occasional entertaining.

As the room is in use at all times of the day, light colours and restrained patterns are a wise choice for walls and fabrics, particularly in a small room.

Good tempered pine
The dining table and chairs in this period house are in old stripped pine, matt varnished for protection.

Commodious dressers either side of the chimney breast cope with toys and games as well as china, glass, cutlery

Wipeable wallcoverings are practical and the designs available are getting better all the time.

Paint is a good alternative. You could try your hand at one of the fashionable paint techniques such as sponging or dragging. They do, however, take time and trouble, so make sure you use washable paint or protect the walls with a clear matt varnish.

and linen. The flooring is a practical vinyl with the mellow look of old country tiles.

The baby's cushion – a foam shape, covered in a wipeable fabric with ribbon ties, is a good way of making a high chair more comfortable.

Flooring should be hardwearing. Vinyl or cork are sensible options although both are rather unfriendly for children who like to play on the floor, so add an inexpensive, washable rug. If you prefer carpet, use a rug to protect it from spills and choose short pile carpet in a discreet pattern or a twist pile in a plain mid-range colour.

Sturdy tables and chairs are essential in a room used by children for play or homework. And you need ample storage for toys, games and books as well as for table linen, china and cutlery.

Lighting needs to be flexible – the ideal is a combination of background and direct light, which can be lowered when you want to create a warm pool of light on the table.

When planning a family dining room, remember that adaptability is the key. The challenge is to make a pleasant environment not just for eating in, but for all kinds of family activities.

Day into night

This very practical room (above) has a sealed wood floor and walls covered with tile-effect vinyl.

It is easily and inexpensively transformed for a special occasion (right). Muslin (or any other cheap, loosely woven cotton) draped over a pole softens the window and the functional table is dressed up with a floor-length tablecloth under a smaller lace one.

The rise-and-fall light is pushed up and switched off, leaving candles to create an intimate mood.

scale: 1 square = 1 metre

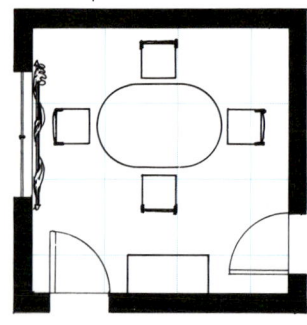

FAMILY STYLE

Furniture for the family dining room has to be chosen with care. It should be tough enough to survive everyday treatment *and* good looking enough to live up to special occasions.

Chairs and tables Small children have to climb to reach the seats of standard height dining chairs. Make sure the chairs are sturdily constructed and do not easily tip or tilt or have hinges that can pinch small fingers.

Ideally, the table should have a fairly indestructible surface. Think about one with a laminated top or an old solid wood farmhouse table which can take a little rough treatment.

A plain table can always be dressed up with a floor length cloth when you entertain. It's easy to make your own or you can use a patterned double sheet or a cotton Indian bedspread. You can cover a plain cloth with a smaller, lacy one, as in the picture opposite, for a pretty effect.

If your dining table is made of a fine wood with a polished surface, protect it with a felt undercloth, an old blanket or a special table pad, and keep it covered with a top cloth for everyday use. A waterproof, wipeable fabric is an invaluable surface when children are indulging in such satisfying but messy activities as painting and modelling with Plasticine. A PVC top cloth is ideal and needs no hemming. If you have to join two pieces to cover a wide table, make an overlap seam.

Storage It's difficult to keep a well-used family dining room tidy. The best approach is to have plenty of handy storage, so you can make a quick transformation at mealtimes, sweeping toys and games out of sight and setting the table with the minimum of fuss.

Instead of a conventional sideboard, you may prefer to opt for a more flexible storage system, cupboards and/or a chest-of-drawers.

A large dresser is useful and takes up very little floor space; use the bottom cupboard to conceal children's clutter, the drawers for linen and cutlery, and open shelves, high out of harm's way, to display china.

Another good storage idea is a built-in windowseat with a lift-up top, or cupboards underneath for tidying away children's toys and games out of sight.

Time spent working out just what is the best solution for your needs helps make your dining room a pleasant place for the whole family.

BRIGHT IDEA

Padded table mats are practical, attractive and easy to make. Sandwich a layer of machine washable wadding between two pieces of cotton; tack and quilt in a simple diamond pattern, then bind the edge with 25mm bias binding in a matching or contrasting colour. Use with a cork mat for hot dishes.

Part of the action
There are obvious advantages to having the dining room close to the kitchen, particularly if it has a large hatch between the two rooms.

You can keep an eye on children playing in the dining room while working in the kitchen. Here the children are 'helping' with the cooking, without getting underfoot in the kitchen.

In addition to the obvious bonus of being able to hand heavy dishes and plates through the hatch, the cook needn't feel isolated from guests when preparing food for a dinner party.

◁ Rainbow colours

Bench seating is a good alternative to chairs in a family dining room – you can squeeze three children into the space taken up by two chairs.

Here a bench is teamed with two bentwood chairs, and bright, washable cushions are added for comfort.

The painted floor is an inexpensive way to 'lift' plain wooden boards. Patterns can be abstract like this one, or geometric, or you can stencil a design.

Use oil-based paint on a well-prepared wooden floor, and protect your design with several coats of clear matt polyurethane varnish.

▽ Elegant and functional

This well-proportioned room is large enough for a big, solid dining table in the centre and still has plenty of play space.

In a good-sized, light room such as this, a rich, darkish colour scheme works well without being overpowering.

BRIGHT IDEA

A **dimmer switch** is ideal in a dining room, allowing you to change the atmosphere simply by adjusting the light level.

There are a variety of controls on the market, including touchplates, rotary or slide switches and even automatic ones that react to the amount of natural light outside. Energy saving, relatively inexpensive and simple to install, they are available in various styles from traditional brass, standard white or chrome to brightly coloured plastic.

Eating in the Kitchen

Recently, there's been a move back to thinking of the kitchen as the traditional heart of the family home – a friendly place in which to eat and chat, feel warm and relaxed.

Even if you have a living/dining area, or a separate formal dining room, using it involves endless trips back and forth, and at least one meal a day usually ends up being taken in the kitchen. Eating breakfast there is convenient and quick. And if there is room on the table to open a newspaper or put a portable television, so much the better.

With young families, peace of mind dictates that meals take place in the washable, less destructable surroundings of a kitchen. Table space is also useful so children can play within view while you're working.

Today, every magazine and home interiors book shows attractive kitchen/ dining rooms, many with an informal, 'farmhouse' feel. With space at a premium, kitchens and kitchen/dining areas are often the only place to eat, for family and friends alike. But instead of being steamy, smelly and unattractive, today's kitchens have all the advantages that modern technology can offer. Extractor fans remove cooking smells and steam, a wide range of light fittings provide pleasant – even romantic – alternatives to fierce fluorescent glare, and many hard-wearing modern floor and wall coverings, designed especially for kitchens, are as pretty as those used in the living room. There are kitchen units designed to look like countrified dressers, ones with classic mouldings and panels, and others which have a smart Italian look.

The heart of the home
A relaxed, well-organized kitchen makes meals a pleasure to prepare and eat.

THE KITCHEN/DINING ROOM

Combined kitchen/dining rooms have become very appropriate to the modern, informal way of life. The problem is many houses haven't been built this way! The answer is to see how knocking down or moving a wall can open up space usefully – combining a scullery and back room in a turn-of-the-century terrace, for example; knocking together a small kitchen and pokey dining room, or removing a wall between a kitchen and passage.

Separate areas In a kitchen big enough to accommodate a free-standing table (with enough space for chairs and for

people to move around) providing a separate eating area is no problem. Bear in mind that the table can double as an extra work surface. More people can fit round a round table than a rectangular one of similar surface area; on the other hand, rectangular tables with drop sides can be pushed against the wall for everyday use, then pulled out for family meals or expanded for dinner parties.

Define the dining area There are various ways to 'dress up' the eating area so that it seems more like a dining room. Choose wallpaper or paint which contrasts with the kitchen area. You can

change the floor covering too – perhaps using warm, attractive, vinyl-coated cork tiles in the cooking area, with matting or a rug to define the dining area (make sure the rug is non-slip). A simple solution for night-time entertaining is to use clever lighting to block off the cooking area (see opposite).

A fan will help get rid of cooking smells, either by circulating the air through charcoal filters or extracting it through an outside wall.

Surface charm Tables and counter tops should be dual purpose, serving both as work surfaces and places to eat. There are several good, all-round surface

Here are two approaches to knocking together two pokey rooms to create a long narrow room with clearly defined dining and kitchen areas.

◁ *All-purpose table*
Families with young children would probably prefer to place the table at the window end of the rectangular room, so the children can play and do homework in daylight. In this countrified room an old settle with a lift-up seat makes it easy to sweep away children's toys when the room needs to be tidy.

A light quarry tile floor, pine furniture and fittings and white paint throughout keep the room fresh and unified. As the kitchen end is rather dark, electric light needs to be kept on most of the time.

▽ *Cook's choice*
If the kitchen/dining area doesn't have to double as a playroom, the cook would probably opt to have a U-shaped kitchen area at the window end, with a more formal eating area at the other end of the room.

In this elegant treatment (floor plan right), the walls and floor are treated differently in each area. The lighting emphasizes the difference too: a rise-and-fall lamp creates an intimate pool of light on the table, while a dimmer switch will throw the cooking area into shadow.

BRIGHT IDEA

A rise-and-fall light on a pulley or spring-coil system is ideal over a dining table. Raised, it provides general working light; lowered, it creates an intimate pool of light for eating, particularly if you use dimmer switches on lights in the cooking area.

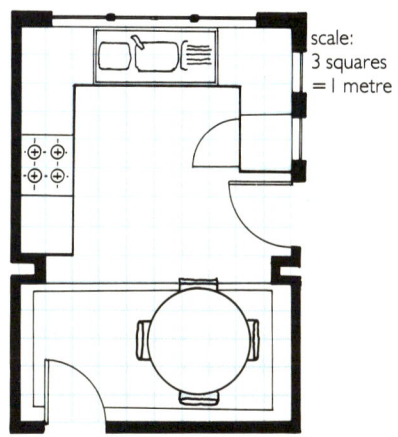

scale:
3 squares
= 1 metre

materials. Stripped, scrubbed wood is practical, traditional and pleasing, and so is oiled teak, beech or maple. Melamine is certainly practical, and its somewhat clinical look is easy to dress up with pretty place mats or tablecloths. Tiled counter tops and tables can be given the same treatment and, of course, there are many attractive tiles from which to choose. (If you use heat-proof tiles, you can put hot casseroles straight on to them.)

If you are lucky enough to have slate or marble surfaces, there is no need to disguise them. They are, however, expensive, heavy materials.

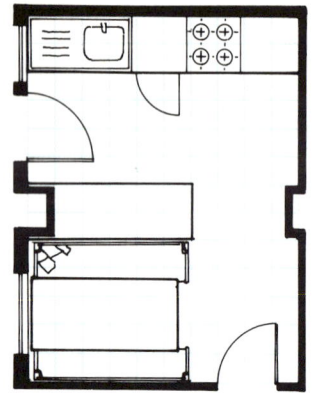

△ **Movable feast**
For a banquette effect that is cheaper and more flexible than a built-in unit, combine a pair of high-back benches, or settles, and a free-standing table with a single, central support (floor plan right).

scale: 3 squares = 1 metre

▷ **Sitting pretty**
Firmly fixed, this purpose-built banquette was cleverly designed to use every inch of the small space available. There is seating on three sides, and the table is angled to allow a clear passageway through the room as well as an extra seat. Although part of the kitchen, the dining area has an elegant and separate feeling.

BANQUETTE SEATING

Built-in, upholstered bench seating is used in restaurants for a very good reason – more people can squeeze in than at separate tables and chairs. The same solution is equally sensible in the home as it makes good use of space, especially in an alcove, corner or recess. Seating can be on two sides, or U-shaped, on three sides, and an extra chair can always be pushed up to the end of the table when needed.

The sense of physical enclosure is pleasing, and helps keep energetic children in place. Storage can be built under flip-top seating. Add seat and back cushions for comfort, and make sure they are washable. Banquette tables should have a single central support, or the kind of cross-over legs which do not make getting in and out difficult.

Because it usually has to be purpose-built, banquette seating is expensive, unless you can build it yourself. Less expensively you can improvize with garden seats, settles or converted pews, made comfortable with cushions. When adding cushions, leave enough space between the seat and underside of the table for your knees.

◁ **High-level charm**
Purpose-built but very simple counter space combines work surface and eating area in one clean, continuous flow. Under-counter storage is also dual-purpose: half for bar stools, half, behind the vertical panel, for the plumbing and drainage pipes as well as the usual collection of under-sink cleaning equipment.

COUNTER-TOP DINING

Generally, counters work best if they are backed up by alternative eating space elsewhere – a table in the living or dining room. Even so, counters offer plenty of scope for creativity when it comes to eating arrangements.

As well as the traditional, straight counter top with a couple of stools tucked underneath, manufacturers of fitted kitchens now offer a range of counters specifically for sitting and eating at. They are positioned at the end of peninsular storage units or free-standing island work spaces; or they project out into the room at right angles to the run of units along the wall.

These counters can be rounded or angular, and some are widened out to feel more like relaxed places for eating. The number of people who can fit around the table area together varies according to size and design, but if two people can sit at right angles, it makes for a feeling of companionship.

The standard work surface height of kitchen units is higher than the normal dining table height. Bar stools or other high-legged chairs are fine for adults but, unless they have arms and high footrest bars, they are tricky for young children.

Wall counters If the only solution is to build a counter along a blank wall, try to brighten the 'view' with a pinboard. You can put up an ever-changing gallery of postcards, pictures torn from magazines, cartoons or reminders.

Counter thoughts

☐ It is much pleasanter to eat at a counter that faces into a room or looks out of a window than one that faces a blank wall.

☐ Open shelves above a counter used for eating are more friendly than a closed cupboard.

☐ Ideally, space below a counter should allow for tucked-in stools and knees.

☐ A small potted plant or vase of flowers on the counter provides an instant 'dining table' centre-piece.

△ **Low-level comfort**
For families with young children or elderly people, lower-level counters and chairs are safer and more comfortable. Here, the counter is fixed to the back of a standard run of units. The lower level means that children's toys and painting materials don't get mixed up with vegetables and dirty dishes.

SPACE SAVERS

While every small kitchen usually has some horizontal work surface, using this for dining is easier said than done. If it is not already crowded with storage jars, utensils or small appliances, chances are it is where you prepared the meal, and eating amidst your own potato peelings, as it were, can be very off putting.

The other problem is that of seating. In a very small kitchen, the space beneath the work surface is usually occupied by cupboards, and there is none left for stools or chairs, let alone knees.

There are solutions, some traditional and others more 'high-tech'. Most ingenious are pull-out table tops, available from some manufacturers of fitted kitchen units. When closed, the table tops are indistinguishable from drawers: when open, they cantilever out, providing a surface equal to the depth of the counter top, and large enough for one, perhaps two, place settings. These pull-out table tops do have a slight out-on-a-limb feeling, and do not make terribly good work surfaces. An improved version, offered in some fitted kitchen styles, is a pull-out table top with legs attached. Again, the top, when not in use, fits inside the unit, while the legs are flush with the surface. When pulled out, the 'table' feels relatively stable, because the legs provide firm support.

More traditional are the fold-down tables, which are wall hung and therefore out of the way when not in use. They range in size from the one-person mini-table to a two- or even four-person table.

△ Clear the decks
Neat fold-down tables are available ready-made. Folding chairs save space too, and can be hung on the wall to clear the decks when necessary.

△ A fold-down table
In a small kitchen, a semi-circular, fold-down table doubles as a space-saving work surface and a comfortable dining table. Hard-wearing floor tiles have been continued up the wall and open shelving provides easily accessible storage.

Kitchen with a Country Look

The aim of the designer of this large kitchen/breakfast room was to combine a country feel with town sophistication. The heavy, rustic look of solid wood was out. Instead, cool white and a degree of formality have been combined with rural materials – old pine, copper, brass and enamelled steel.

The good-size farmhouse table with its thick butcher's block top provides extra workspace for food preparation and can also be used for informal meals. It has a shelf underneath for those utensils which need to be close to hand.

An old-fashioned clothes airer *fitted on pulleys makes getting at heavy utensils easier than a fixed frame.*

Knobs and hinges
The clinical look of all-white units is softened by brass knobs and hinges and a planked door finish.

Ceiling-hung utensils
An iron frame fixed to the ceiling is a good way to store decorative but less frequently used utensils.

Planked ceiling
Tongued and grooved boards – to match cupboard doors – are painted sea green and make an attractive and durable ceiling finish.

Cupboards to fit
Fitting small cupboards above an extra large fridge like this neatly completes a run of top units.

Delft-style tiles
Blue and white tiles between floor and wall units give the room a country touch.

Grouping pictures
Arranging pictures and an interesting choice of objects in a fairly formal group looks decorative but uncluttered.

Farmhouse table
An old wooden table is less formal than a laminate one and is practical for preparing and eating meals.

Free-standing appliances
To avoid too streamlined a look, choose free-standing appliances aligned with a run of units instead of built-in ones.

A Rural Setting

The mood of this country house kitchen/dining room is appealingly relaxed and friendly.

Dark green units blend with the trees and plants outside and, during the day, glass doors confuse the boundary between the outside world and inside the house.

The kitchen area is well away from that used for eating, with a door to the outside making a convenient division between the two activities.

At night, a rise-and-fall light over the table adds to the feeling of separation from the busy, working end of the room.

When the curtains are drawn and all lights except those over the table are dimmed, the dining area becomes a cosy focus for the room.

Glass doors
Full-length glazed doors give a kitchen an airy feel in the day. Long curtains can be drawn at night to give a cosier feel.

Cupboards plus shelves
A combination of fitted units and open shelves relieves a solid run of units, particularly those with a dark finish.

Clothes airer
Old-fashioned airers are still available and provide a good way to show off masses of dried flowers. Pull the airer up and down to change the arrangement.

Formal table
It is still possible to find inexpensive old dining tables in mahogany, which are a better choice in a room used for semi-formal meals than a kitchen table.

Pendant light
A rise-and-fall fitting – ideally on a separate wiring circuit from other lighting – is a good choice in a kitchen/dining room. This Edwardian design is in sympathy with the old table.

Unit finish
Dark green kitchen units are a good alternative to natural wood in a country kitchen and they work well with a mahogany table.

Garden view
Siting the main working area under a window gives a feeling of actually being in the garden.

Light and Airy Kitchen-Diner

The rather long, narrow space created by extending the kitchen has been broken up visually to provide two separate, but linked areas.

The space nearest the patio doors is devoted to dining. It features natural materials – exposed brickwork and old pine; over the table is a period-style pendant light fitting.

The 'work' end of the room has a conventional arrangement of fitted units. Laminated cupboards and worktops would destroy the mellow look of the room. The bright, dragged paint finish, plus light stone-coloured tiles, separate this end visually without creating a jarring impression.

Choosing the same flooring throughout successfully links the two parts of the room as do a variety of country-style decorations such as pretty flower prints on the wall and floral patterned pieces of china.

Display space
The open plate rack and glass-doored cupboards are ideal for displaying china and ornaments. They also soften the line of the work units.

Indoor garden
Trailing plants add to the rustic charm of the kitchen and help to bring a garden feel to the room.

Ceiling contrast
A painted wooden ceiling fitted with efficient downlighters defines the work area; a smoothly plastered ceiling marks out the dining area.

Paint effect
The obvious way to give a country look to a kitchen is to fit natural wood units. By painting them, using a drag technique, you can achieve a lighter, more unusual effect.

Room divider
A peninsular unit with inset hob makes a natural division between working and eating areas.

Double grid
The distinctive grid design of the tiled worktop is echoed on a larger scale in the terracotta floor tiles.

Streamlined Simplicity

Industrial designer Barry Weaver removed a dividing wall between two rooms to create this kitchen/diner. The colour scheme he chose has a calming and unifying effect. The cream walls and ceiling, natural floor tiles and plain beech units contrast with the rough exposed brickwork and shiny chrome.

Plate rack
This old-fashioned plate rack matches the plain wood of the kitchen units. Placed across the window, its widely spaced bars allow the light through even when the rack is fully loaded.

Hang up your pans
A chrome bar, supported at both ends and in the centre, makes a handy storage rack for all sorts of attractive kitchen utensils – hang them from S-shaped butcher's hooks or hooked chrome rings.

Fascia boards
Most kitchen unit suppliers provide matching fascia boards for filling areas such as the space between wall cupboards and the ceiling. You can use them to back the wall between the worktop and cupboards. Tongue and groove panelling would work equally well in a natural wood kitchen.

Tiled surfaces
Heavy-duty floor tiles are also used to tile the work surfaces. They are heat and scratch resistant, and are easy to clean.

Two into one
This kitchen/diner was originally two small rooms. A wall was replaced by a steel joist and the fireplace removed leaving the side walls of the chimney breast, which created an awkward alcove. The problem was solved by continuing the worktop across the alcove, which is fitted with shelves and makes a good storage area.

Shades of Blue and Pine

Nothing can beat a well-planned kitchen and if you take the trouble to design one you will reap the benefits for a long time afterwards. Whether putting together a quick snack or preparing something special, the task will be much easier if you have a kitchen that is a pleasure to work in.

This spacious kitchen looks as though it has taken a lot of time and money to design but the rules are simple: panelled pine kitchen units and a predominant use of blue to give the kitchen its colour. Other colours are not allowed to intrude and spoil the overall look: the gentle use of grey feels like a reflection of the blue.

Blue in abundance
Utensils and napery have been chosen in blue and white – from the faded shades of the wall-hung plates to the intense, deep blue of the casseroles. For a similar look choose a colour that won't date and that you won't tire of.

Cleverly boxed
Unsightly pipes are cleverly concealed by timber tongued-and-grooved panels painted blue. More timber panelling and pine is used to place directional lighting and an extractor fan above the hob.

Space for display
The combination of glazed doors and open shelves allows the blue and white crockery to be displayed attractively rather than hidden away behind cupboard doors. Glazed doors cut down on dusting!

Suitable seating
Dining chairs with rush seats are painted white and used as seating around the breakfast bar. The chairs also fit in with the colour scheme used throughout the room. If you need lots of workspace in your kitchen, folding chairs could be a better alternative as they can be moved out of the way.

Breakfast bar
This breakfast bar is simply an extension on two sides of the gas hob and kitchen unit. It can seat four people comfortably and takes maximum advantage of space by using an area that would probably otherwise be wasted.

Light conservatory
The streaming bright light from the conservatory travels into the kitchen and brings life by adding contrasting light and dark shadows. The blue of the kitchen is faintly echoed in the conservatory but an airy feel, leafy plants and white garden furniture make the conservatory seem an enticing extension of the kitchen.

Grey compromise
Grey and white tiles laid chequerboard-fashion on the floor and a finely striped grey wallpaper form a restful link between the blue paintwork and the white worktops.

Dining with Nostalgia

Collecting memorabilia is something that most people enjoy but finding a place to store or display these collections can be a problem.

Here, an eclectic mixture of objects is carefully displayed and is used as an integral part of this room's decor. The result is an atmosphere that is a pleasant mixture of warmth and cosiness. The room is clearly someone's pride and joy.

Everything in the room seems to have been collected over time giving the room a style that is truly individual. The careful arrangement of furniture and ornaments helps to avoid a cluttered appearance.

Decorated pine
Doors on the pine cupboard have been given a personal touch with stick-on patterns in embossed metal. An alternative would be to make up your own stencil and paint it on to the cupboards.

On the wall
A collection of plates and bowls is displayed on the wall – a space-saving and attractive solution if space for shelves is limited or if you want to create an eye-catching display.

Papered door
The wallpaper is carried over on to the door to create a feeling of continuity. The paper on the door is protected by a coat of clear polyurethane varnish. The door mouldings are picked out in a bue-green that echoes the paper.

Nicely framed
Framed pictures of varying sizes and shapes sit comfortably together on this wall, underpinned by the chest of drawers that in turn holds a small exhibition of treasures including an antique clock and a 1930s-style bust.

Easy storage
Large pine cupboards give this dining room plenty of storage space but notice that the storage is unconventional for a dining room – combining a chest of drawers with large cupboards. An old wardrobe that blends with the style of your room could be fitted with shelves and used just as successfully.

Table focus
The table setting breaks away from the overall period feel of this room and, by using strong colours, manages to create a dramatic focal point. A green tablecloth would have blended in with the surroundings, but the spotlessly white cloth acts as a perfect foil for boldly-patterned china.

Flower sense
Three simple flower arrangements on the chest of drawers underline the natural feel of the room. In keeping with the rest of the room, there is nothing tailored or uniform about them – the vases are all different and the flower display is unique to each vase.

Pine furniture
The stripped pine of the chair, cupboards and chests give the room a warm, 'cottagey' atmosphere. The fact that all the wood has been left in its natural state enhances this feeling. The only wooden furniture that's not in pine are the mahogany dining chairs – but these help to emphasize the room's focal point.

Off-the-Peg Dining Suites

Furnishing a dining room needs careful consideration, as a special atmosphere has to be created within a functional framework. Dining-room furniture needs to look good, be comfortable, and yet be sturdy enough to withstand hard wear over the years.

Choosing furniture that's right for your dining room is a very personal affair; before you start considering particular suites, you really need to look closely at how the room is likely to be used. Do you entertain frequently, so that additional chairs and an extendable table would be useful? If the room is to be used for other purposes, will the table be suitable for, say, a child's painting session, or as a surface for a sewing machine? If your dining area is small, will your choice of table, chairs and side furniture leave sufficient space for access?

Styles range from excellent reproductions of antiques to ultra-modern designs, the more extremes of which owe little to convention. You will obviously need to choose a style that suits the way you normally dine. For formal entertaining you may want to set the scene with a traditional elegance. If most of your meals are relaxed family affairs and you like to have friends in for casual suppers, your style will be impeded if the setting is too stiffly formal. A modern classic may appeal, but take care to choose a style that won't date. If children will be using the dining room, well-oiled wood gives a robust surface or a wipe-clean finish such as a laminate will be a practical choice.

Extending range
Handsome, self-assembly dining furniture, practical for family meals yet stylish enough for entertaining. A flexible range of cupboards, drawers and glazed dresser tops can be bought separately, and will allow you to build up matching extras piece by piece to complete your dining suite.

△ **Formal charm**
This mellowed pine suite is a fine example of modern craftsmanship. Upholstered chairs are especially comfortable for mealtimes: these have been given practical tie-on covers.

▽ **Elegantly classic**
This modern suite, with extending octagonal table and high-backed chairs, sets a sophisticated scene; the elegant good looks would blend well with a traditional or modern scheme.

FORMAL SETTING

There are many good-quality reproductions of antique dining furniture made by craftsmen using traditional methods and designs. Well-made veneered furniture will stand the test of time, but avoid cheap veneers where the layer is so thin it won't last.

A good modern style will also grace a formal setting. Designs range from trend-setting Italian furniture to more conventional classics in natural beech, chrome and glass, and moulded plastics. If you're tempted by a style that breaks with tradition, make sure it really is comfortable and that it's a design you won't tire of.

BASIC DESIGNS

Tables are available in many different finishes – solid wood and veneers, lacquered or laminated, metal, glass, even marble – and you can choose from a variety of shapes. They can extend in inventive ways, so it's advisable to check the operation in the showroom.

As dinner is often a variable feast, your table should be able to extend to include usual entertaining needs as well as family affairs. The shape of the table will affect conversation; round tables in particular create a pleasant social group, and everyone can reach all the condiments, though a large round table isn't the easiest of shapes to accommodate.

A long rectangular table may fit neatly into your room, but the shape

encourages neighbourly chat rather than general conversation. Try to choose a table whose legs aren't awkwardly sited so they restrict diners' leg room.

Chairs come in a wide selection of high- or low-backed shapes and different materials. Test them thoroughly; they must give good lumbar support for long

△ *Traditional taste*
While there is nothing quite like the real thing, there are many good reproduction antique suites on the market. If you want carver chairs, make sure they slip nicely under the table.

eating sessions. Before you buy, sit on the chairs at the table to ensure they are a comfortable height and check that carver arms will fit easily under the table. If you are adding cushions to hard chairs, make sure this won't make them too high for the table.

Upholstered chairs are usually very comfortable and would be ideal for long dining sessions, but do need re-covering from time to time. Protect the fabric with a stain repellent, or fit loose covers: a sensible precaution if you have children.

Dining extras As well as your basic suite of table and chairs, you will probably need a surface for serving and space for storing necessities. Many manufacturers offer a range of matching furniture which includes dressers, sideboards and corner cabinets which blend in with the basic table and chairs.

◁ *Design dining*
There are several reproductions of the comfortable Bauhaus chair. The low backs and light design make a suite like this a good choice for a modern dining/sitting room. Square or round tables are particularly convivial shapes, as the entire company can converse together.

▽ Pine design
Budget-priced modern pine chairs and tables are a practical choice for family use, as the wood generally has a polyurethane coating for easy care.

Off-the-peg suites such as this can look informally cottage-like or be dressed up. The same suite of furniture is shown in the view below, with an alternative decoration to set a completely different dining scene.

INFORMAL DESIGN

You may not have the space or inclination to set a dining scene of traditional elegance. If you would prefer a more casually relaxed mood for family suppers or informal get-togethers, consider pale Scandinavian pine or beech, natural wicker, or a laminate. For a rustic atmosphere, light oak or farmhouse-style pine would look appropriately chunky; many ranges have matching dressers. Pine that's been given a mellowed finish will cost more but has a softer, more natural glow than the rather raw look of new pine that's simply been polyurethaned. Avoid polished surfaces that need constant cossetting. Glass can be noisy, and shows smears. A laminate or oiled or varnished wood will eliminate the need for mats except for very hot dishes.

Self-assembly would suit a low budget. Finishes range from white or coloured laminate to solid wood. There are also reasonable veneers of attractively grained wood like ash, either natural or stained black or grey.

DINING ROOM CHECKLIST
Before you shop, note key points:
☐ **How much you want to spend** If your budget is tight, consider self-assembly.
☐ **Room size and shape** Take a scale drawing to the showroom. Allow for access round the outskirts so guests aren't pinned in their seats.
☐ **The style and atmosphere** you want to create. Bear in mind existing features that could affect choice, and other purposes for which the room is used.
☐ **Your basic dining needs** Size of family, plus possible extension for larger gatherings. Allow generous elbow room.
☐ **Side furniture**, for serving and storage requirements. If you want to concentrate initially on basic table and chairs, look for a range you can add to later on.
☐ **Special needs** Choose robust surfaces if you have children.

BRIGHT IDEA

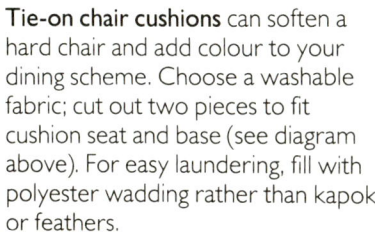

Tie-on chair cushions can soften a hard chair and add colour to your dining scheme. Choose a washable fabric; cut out two pieces to fit cushion seat and base (see diagram above). For easy laundering, fill with polyester wadding rather than kapok or feathers.

▽ *Victorian style*
This reproduction furniture borrows inspiration from a not-too-distant past: antiqued pine styled by craftsmen to an original Victorian design.

△ *Family dining*
Low-cost dining furniture with a wipe-clean laminate finish would be a good choice when children are young. A tablecloth adds personal style.

△ Dining space
If you have to entertain occasionally in your living room or don't have space for a dining table, a gateleg which can also double as a console is a good choice. Take care if you are considering an extending table. Make sure you choose a style that's easy to operate, and convenient. Some extensions have to be stored separately, which could be a real nuisance if space is limited.

BRIGHT IDEA

Drop-in seats can be covered for a quick change of decor. Choose a washable material; cut out enough to cover seat and sides and extend 5cm underneath seat base. Hem edges, then zigzag stitch over a 10cm length of elastic to gather the corners.

Versatile Dining

Few people have the space nowadays to devote an entirely separate room in their home to dining, and nothing else. In most homes, whether flats or houses, space is at a premium and the chances are that you will have no choice but to make the dining room double as something else as well.

The kitchen/dining room is – not surprisingly, given the close association between cooking and eating – the most popular partnership. But there are several other possibilities. These include the dining/living room, the dining/guest room, the dining/work room, and even the dining room/hall – often a good solution in converted flats where halls can be positively spacious in relation to some of the other rooms. At the drop of a table leaf and the unfolding of a few chairs, you can accommodate all the family and friends you want.

The most common arrangement of all is the dining area which is no more than a corner of another room. More often than not, this is the kitchen or the living room.

Round in circles

A circular dining table is one of the most sociable arrangements for eating, but takes up a lot of space. This one has two drop leaves, either one or both of which can be used, which makes it a very versatile solution to the problem of seating family and friends for dinner without taking up too much space permanently in the kitchen.

▽ ▷ *Dropping in*
A simple drop-leaf table such as this makes for maximum versatility. An oval table with two leaves which fold away easily, it will readily seat up to six people, or you can put up just one leaf and use it as extra work space or for supper for two.

GETTING EQUIPPED

The secret of a successful versatile approach to dining is to make the most of the space you have available and to use it sensibly. And that means both maintaining a flexible attitude and, possibly even more important, finding the right sort of furniture which lends itself to this treatment.

Perhaps, for example, you want a dinng table that doesn't look like one most of the time. This means being able to use it easily for something else – as a console table in the hall or for stacking books, say, though this does mean you need somewhere convenient to move them to when you use the table for eating. It helps too if you don't have to surround it with chairs all the time, which is where folding or stacking chairs, which are great space savers, come in useful.

Even if you do have a completely separate dining area, you may not always want to cater for the same number of people. Four people can feel uncomfortably out of place sitting round a huge table that would happily accommodate ten, and – conversely – eight people bumping elbows crammed around too small a table are unlikely to feel at ease.

Do, if you have the space, look for a dining table whose size can be altered by adding an extension or extra leaves.

▷ *Flexible seating arrangements*
Both these tables lend themselves to versatile seating arrangements, depending on how you set them up.

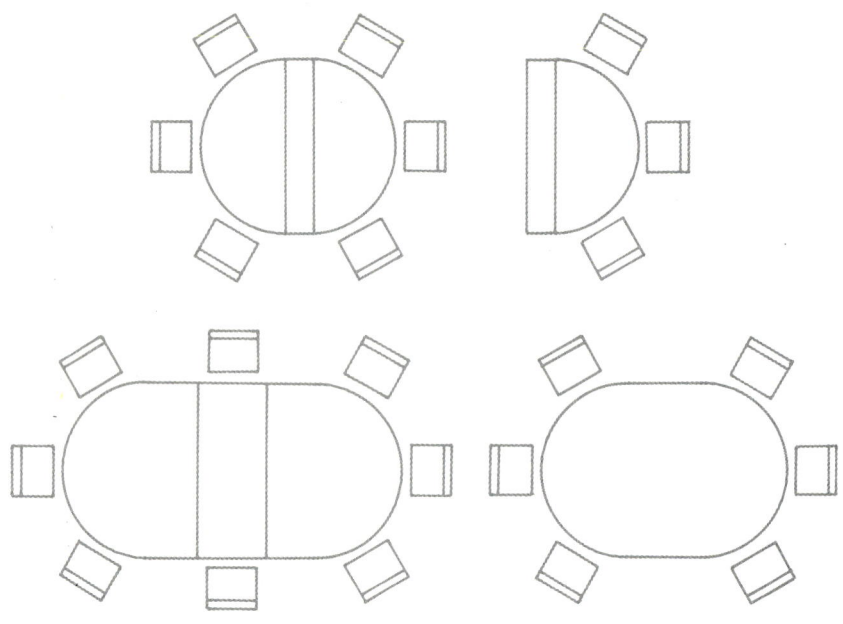

◁ **Practical styling**
Combining easy practicality
with elegant styling, this
dining table is 1624mm long
and extends to 2328mm
with an extension leaf, when
it will seat eight people. A
traditional-style mahogany
table, this is suitable for a
dining area as well as an
entirely separate dining
room.

▷ **Doubling up**
This simple drop-leaf kitchen table seats
two or three people when positioned
against the wall. It can also be extended
to provide an extra storage surface or
to seat up to six people for an informal
supper.

AN OPEN AND SHUT CASE

Here are two good ideas where space is limited. A butler's table (right) is a folding table-cum-tray on legs, which can be used for a cosy supper or a quick snack. A trestle table (above) can be stored away beside a cupboard or even under a bed and brought out when you want to entertain.

▽ **On the shelf**

This sliding shelf in a tiny, well thought-out, custom-built kitchen can be pulled out to provide an extra surface, whether for working, for storage, or on which to grab a quick breakfast or a hurried snack on the run.

△ Swivel top
A large Victorian dining table on a central pedestal can be stored with its top swivelled flat against a wall, where it takes little space.

▽ The story unfolds . . .
This simple pine dining table can be folded up into a special wall recess. The ceiling light is on a pulley system and can also be raised out of the way.

IMPROMPTU DINING
It is nice to be able to set up table and eat virtually anywhere in the home when the fancy takes you. The kitchen is the most obvious choice, but what about a cosy supper in front of the television; a romantic breakfast *à deux* in the bedroom; or even an informal dinner with friends in the conservatory (with a view to moving outside, perhaps, if the weather holds)?

A great aid to impromptu dining is to bring out folding varieties of both table and chairs for the occasion, which deals effectively with the problem of where to store all that extra furniture. After use they can be put away in a hall cupboard or even hung out of the way on a wall.

The clear perspex or plexiglass type of folding chair is a particularly good idea, because you can see right through them and they take up very little 'visual' space. The brightly coloured wooden sort is another attractive alternative, particularly if they go well with your decor.

Another solution is to cover all your chairs in a neutral fabric that will go with virtually any colour scheme. Then they can be moved round the house and brought together for dining when needed.

Any part-time dining area will benefit greatly from a trolley or serving cart, which forges the link between eating and cooking. They are also useful as an extra surface for serving and storage.

◁ **Breakfast blues**
An old marble-topped washstand has been converted to form the base of a dresser by fixing a hand-crafted and painted dresser top to the wall above it. This makes a convenient place for a family of three to enjoy a simple breakfast in the corner of an old-fashioned country-style kitchen.

▷ **Kitchen ease**
This modern, multi-functional tiled island unit makes the maximum possible use of space in a small open-plan flat. It forms an ingenious and convenient room divider between the kitchen and living area, as well as doubling as work surface, storage unit and dining area that comfortably seats four or six.

Dining Tables

When choosing a dining table, whether new or second-hand, there are four things to bear in mind: the style of the table, what it is made of, shape and size.

Style should be influenced by the room setting and the chairs you plan to use with it. There is a wide range to choose from, whether you are looking for a practical table to fit into a kitchen/diner or finer furniture for a more formal dining room.

Finish The high cost of solid timber means that most dining tables – whether reproduction or modern in style – are blockboard veneered with a thin layer of wood. Very cheap furniture is sometimes veneered in paper printed to look like wood and with a waterproof seal-

ant. Always check what the veneer is made of and look out for poor finish and chipped edges on wood veneers.

If the table is to be used by children or for other purposes, such as dressmaking or typing, choose a sturdy design and a hard-wearing finish. Melamine is a tough all-purpose surface available in a range of colours. Any wood with a polyurethane varnish is easily wiped clean and is relatively heat resistant. An advantage of solid wood tables is they can be stripped, sanded and refinished if the surface gets badly damaged.

Size and shape The height of a dining table should be between 70-75cm and must be related to the height of the

chairs. Allow 65cm space for each armless chair and 70cm for carvers. A rectangular or oval table must be at least 75cm wide to allow table settings on both sides (see page 85).

Round tables can seat more people more comfortably than square or rectangular tables but when you take into consideration the room the chairs need, they take up more space in a room. A central pedestal leg is less obtrusive than four separate ones. A 900mm diameter table seats 4; 1.2m-1.4m diameter seats 6; 1.5-1.7m seats 8.

Square tables usually seat 4 comfortably, 8 at a push. The legs at the corners can be a problem when seating more than 4.

Rectangular tables seat more people than square tables of the same area. Extension flap(s) or draw leaves present fewer problems with legs than leaves which are inserted centrally. Check the position of the legs in relation to place settings with and without extensions.

Oval tables are a good compromise between round and rectangular tables. They give the most flexible seating, particularly if on a pedestal base, and take up less space than a round table.

FARMHOUSE
A sturdy design usually made from solid pine or oak. Seats 6-8 people depending on size. The thick turned legs support a firm working surface, ideal for kitchen/diners. When choosing chairs to fit note the frame (which often incorporates a drawer) under the table top. Suits the farmhouse or country cottage-look kitchen or dining room – the weight may mark a soft floor covering.

REFECTORY
A 16th century table design with solid panel end supports through which the stetcher bar passes and is pegged. The end panel can be carved or have decorative cut outs and the stretcher bar can be at floor level or midway up. Check to see if people can be seated comfortably at the ends. The table's weight is spread across the wide panel feet so it is less likely to mark a soft floor.

TRESTLE
One of the simplest designs, particularly popular if space is limited as the top and folding legs can be stacked away separately when not in use. The top is usually made from veneered wood, melamine or glass and the legs from chrome or brightly enamelled metal or wood. Check the weight of the top if you intend to stack the table regularly.

MODERN SOLID END
A simple streamlined design which has solid panelled supports linked by a stretcher bar instead of legs. The simple rectangular design means it is usually made from veneered particle board and the clean lines suit a contemporary setting.

ROUND PEDESTAL
A simple circular table with traditional curved tripod legs, or a more streamlined modern design made from glass with chrome legs or veneered wood. Some of the traditional styles have a hinged mechanism which allows the top to tilt vertically so that the table can be pushed against the wall when space is limited.

TWIN PEDESTAL
A long oval table based on Regency designs often has two pedestal legs, with or without a stretcher bar between for extra stability. Some designs incorporate a flip out central panel (see Flip leaf overleaf).

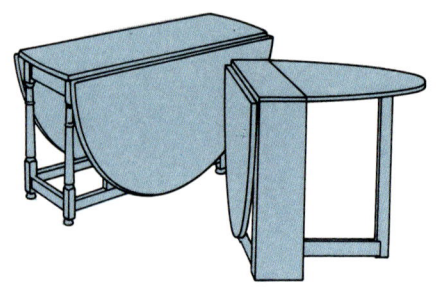

DRUM

A simple circular table supported by four legs. Styles vary from the traditional, with turned legs, to the modern, with chrome or sleek panelled legs. Tops can be made from wood, glass, melamine or marble. Check for leg room if there is a frame under the top.

GATE LEG

Originally an early 17th century Jacobean design, there are both reproduction and modern versions. A lightweight table which is easily moved, the narrow centre panel is traditionally supported on four turned legs, with or without stretcher bars. Modern designs are variations on this style. The deep semi-circular or square flaps are each supported by a leg which swings out from the central section. This versatile table takes up little space when folded and can be used with one or both flaps up. Check the space for knees at the central panel. Made from solid wood or, for modern designs, a wood or melamine veneer.

CENTRE LEAF

These square, circular, oval or rectangular tables can be extended by pulling the table apart and inserting a separate central leaf. Some designs have a second and even a third leaf. The leaves must be stacked carefully to avoid being scratched when not in use and unless they are inserted frequently, there is the problem of the part which is in regular use changing colour with exposure to light and more frequent cleaning.

DROP LEAF

The central panel is considerably larger than that of the gate leg and is either square or rectangular in shape. There is a square or semi-circular flap at one or both ends which is supported by a fold out bracket or slide when raised. The lack of leg support makes the flap unsuitable for a heavy weight, such as a sewing machine or typewriter, but more comfortable for dining as there is no leg to get in the way of knees. Available in both traditional and modern styles.

A Pembroke table is a light elegant drop leaf table with square or shaped drop leaves which are supported, when raised, with hinged fold out brackets. There can be a central pedestal or four legs at the corners of the central panel, under which a drawer is often found.

DRAW LEAF

This traditional rectangular design has extension leaves which fit under the top at each end. When the extensions are pulled out the central panel lowers to fit flush. With age, use and exposure to light the main table top tends to change colour while the leaves remain the same as when new, if they are not extended regularly. The legs may be panelled as here or turned.

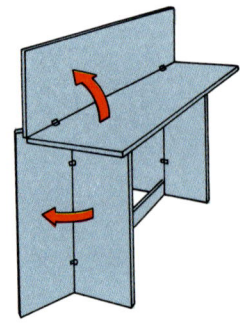

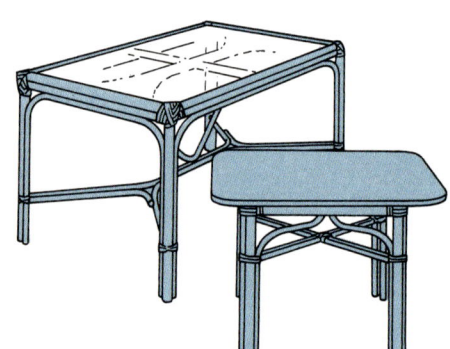

FLIP LEAF

The two halves of the table top pull apart to reveal a central fold out panel which is hinged across the middle and swings out. Some styles have a second panel for greater extension. In this way, a round table turns into an oval and a square into a rectangle.

FOLDING CONSOLE

The central join runs the length of this table so that when it is folded in half it fits neatly against the wall like a console or side table, ideal for a living/dining room. When pulled out and the top opened out the leg divides to support the second half. The decorative brass or silver metal hinges are more obvious in a dark wood.

RATTAN/BAMBOO LOOK

Much bamboo furniture is, in fact, made from steamed and bent beech which has been given a bamboo look. The table top is often made of toughened glass, set into a frame or resting on adhesive pads, which adds to the light open look of the furniture. Wood veneer tops are also available.

Modern Dining Chairs

A universal characteristic of modern styles is lightness, both in weight and visually. This does not mean strength has been sacrificed in most cases, but check the construction carefully if you plan to put the chairs to strenuous use.

Materials As wood has increased in price, designers have experimented with cane, bamboo, metal (especially chrome) and plastics, and these materials have allowed for new designs.

Upholstery Most manufacturers offer a choice of fabrics and, if you ask, many will cover the chairs in your own fabric.

The same design often has a choice of seat style. Fabric, cane, rush and leather are used when appropriate.

Finish As well as natural wood finishes, many modern styles are stained in various colours, lacquered or painted.

Many modern dining chair styles are based on traditional designs but with a cleaner, more streamlined look. Others are completely original in their own right.

The same principles of size, construction, upholstery, etc, outlined on page 85 apply equally to these designs. Bear in mind that many modern tables and chairs are slightly lower than period ones so if you are going to mix your styles check heights carefully.

WOODEN CHAIRS

SQUARE AND ROUNDED UPHOLSTERED
The seat and back panel are fully upholstered and the high back is curved to fit the shape of the body. The curved back has a particularly elegant line. Square legs and stretcher bars make a sturdy chair; slimmer legs without bars give a lighter feel. Also made with a cane back panel and seat and the wood can be natural, stained or lacquered.

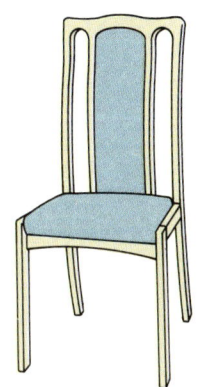

PANELLED UPHOLSTERED
Just the central panel of the high chair back is upholstered, giving it a lighter look. A carver is usually available for most square backed styles.

MODERN LADDERBACK
A streamlined version of the traditional design. Note the higher stretcher bars between the legs which add strength unobtrusively.

Similar in concept is the square or rounded back with a series of narrow or two or three wide vertical bars. The seat is upholstered or rush/cane and the wood is natural, stained or lacquered.

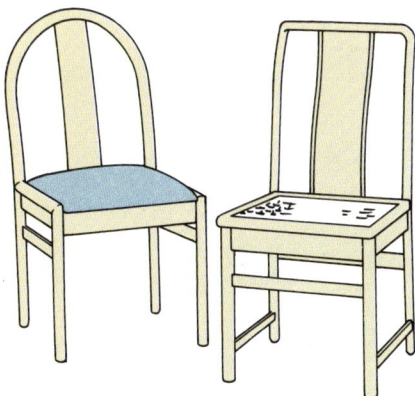

SOLID PANEL BACK
This chair has a mid-height, rounded or squared back with a solid central panel. The seat is cane, rush or upholstered.

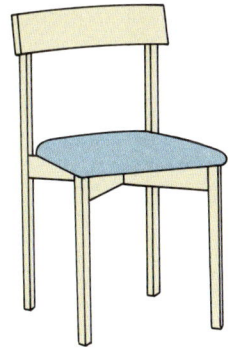

LOW BACK UPHOLSTERED
This very basic chair design is relatively inexpensive. The low curved back panel gives limited support. The seat can be cane, rush or upholstered.

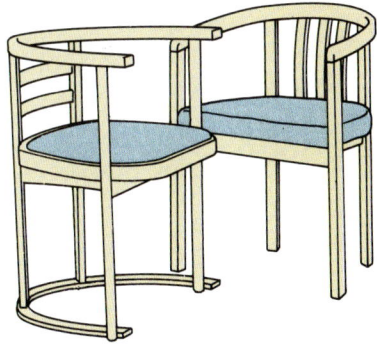

TUB
The low back curves round to form the arms and sometimes there is a similar curved bar at the base into which the legs are fitted. It is also available with conventional legs.

The seat is cane or upholstered and the back panel can be filled with vertical or horizontal bars, or a cane or upholstered central panel.

METAL CHAIRS

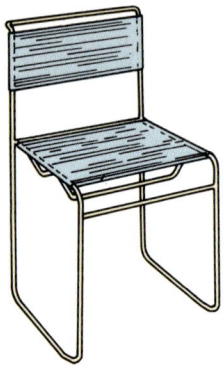 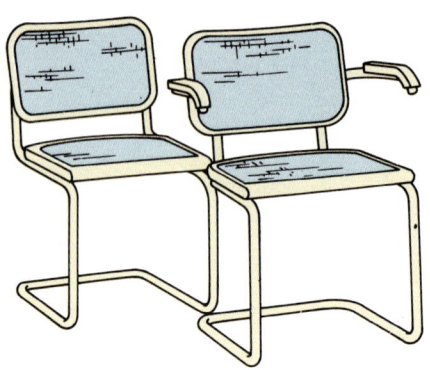 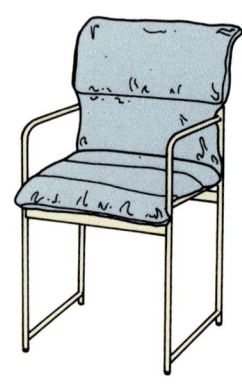

SPAGHETTI
The tubular metal frame comes in a range of bright enamel colours and the seat and back are made from lengths of clear or coloured plastic tubing wound round the frame. The chairs are designed to be stacked one on top of another.

BAUHAUS
A modern classic. The original was leather and chrome but modern versions are made from cane, chrome and wood, which is left natural or stained black. The S shape can be sharply angled or have fluid curves. There is a carver and armless version.

CANVAS AND METAL
Tubular metal framework supports an all-in-one padded canvas seat and back. The covers come in a range of colours and are washable. Simpler versions have a canvas seat and back panel stretched across the frame.

FOLDING CHAIRS

Folding chairs are useful for back up seating although they can, of course, be used as permanent dining furniture. Take care with young children as the chairs may tip and little fingers can get pinched.

WOODEN FOLDING
Available in natural wood finish or stained in various colours. The seat is solid, slatted or cane. Quite bulky when folded.

METAL FOLDING
The tubular metal framework in a range of bright colours has a solid, perforated or mesh seat and back rail. The classic Plia chair is in chrome with a clear acrylic plastic back and seat instead of metal. The legs are joined at the base with a rail front and back or are separate and finished with rubber caps. Folds into a neat narrow shape.

CANVAS AND WOOD
The 'director's' chair frame comes in natural wood or painted in various colours. The canvas seat and back can be replaced when old or stained. They are bulky when folded.

RATTAN/BAMBOO LOOK

Bamboo furniture is no longer exclusively used in the conservatory. It gives a light airy look to a dining room but is relatively fragile and will not stand up to very rough treatment. Much of the furniture sold today is, in fact, made from beech which has been stained and given the bamboo look. Both materials can be steam bent into fluid curves and the intersections are bound with split cane. Painted chairs, usually in pastel colours, are also available. Loose cushions used for the seat and/or back add comfort.

Spoon back An elegant lightweight chair.
Tub The low back rail curves round to form the arms. The space between the rail and seat or just the back panel is completely filled with cane.
Pagoda back A high backed chair with an oriental feel.
Square back A neat low-backed style with cross stretchers to strengthen the legs.

Dining Chairs in Period Styles

Dining chairs and tables are often chosen at the same time, as a matching set, particularly if they are to go into a separate dining room. But do not feel you have to stick rigidly to this – an elegant modern set of chairs can look good with a traditionally designed table. Don't be afraid to mix periods and styles if you think they look right.

When choosing dining chairs bear in mind that they are often put to other uses; for example, at a desk, a sewing table or to provide additional seating in the living room. If your chairs have to serve different purposes make sure they are light enough to move easily and look right in the different settings.

Style Most period designs come in two versions, a carver with arms and an armless chair. Carvers are usually more expensive and take up a lot of space but some people find them more comfortable. A combination, with two carvers at the ends of the table is popular.

Size To work out how many chairs will fit round a table allow about 65cm for armless chairs and 70cm for carvers. The space between the seat and the under side of the table or rim is important. Allow 30-35cm between them and bear in mind that modern tables are usually lower than period styles if you plan to mix them.

Comfort The only way to find out whether a chair is comfortable is to sit on it long enough for any discomfort to make itself felt! Your feet should rest flat on the floor and the seat should be wide and deep enough and should not slope back. The back should be angled to give support when sitting up to a table – some people find a space between the seat and the back support more comfy than a solid back.

The arms of carvers should be shorter than the seat so you can pull the chair right up to the table and preferably they should be lower than the table top so that the chair can be tucked away when not in use. Check that the chair arms are low enough to allow easy movement when eating and that your arms are in a relaxed position when resting.

Upholstery Dining chairs may have the food spilled on them, particularly if there are young children in the family. Drop in seats are easier to replace than fixed upholstery and removable cushion covers are the most practical.

Construction Chairs take a lot of hard wear – being pushed back and forward, tilted and even used to stand on – so look for firm, strong joints. Stretcher bars across the legs also add support and strength.

ELIZABETHAN
A carved panelled back – solid or with a break just above the upholstered seat – and stretcher bars between the legs make these particularly sturdy chairs.

CROMWELLIAN
Strong chairs with leather covered back panel and seat fixed with brass studs. Leather is easily scratched or stained and is expensive to replace.

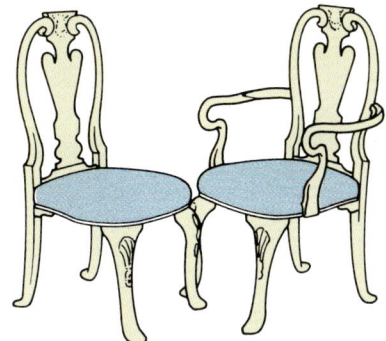

QUEEN ANNE
An elegant chair with elegant cabriole legs without stretcher bars. The high rounded back has a solid central splat and the seat is upholstered.

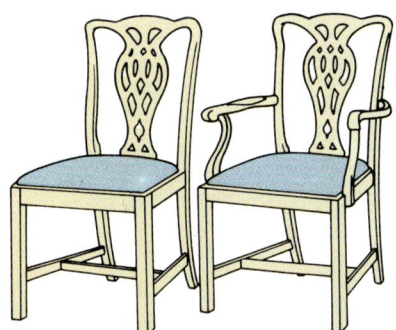

RIBBON BACK CHIPPENDALE
A high square back with a lattice carved central splat gives the chair a lighter look. A drop-in upholstered seat is more easily re-covered than a fixed one.

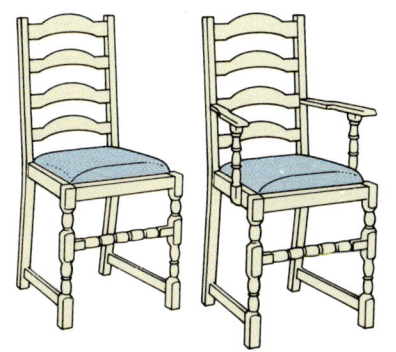

LADDERBACK
The back rungs can be plain or carved; the seat is usually upholstered and dropped in – modern versions can have rush seats. Made in a range of woods.

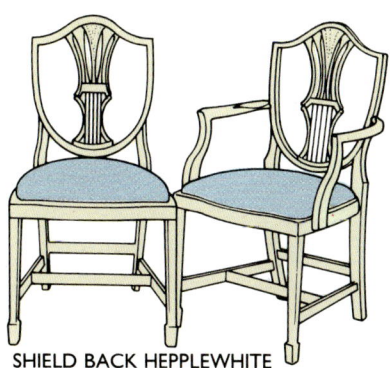

SHIELD BACK HEPPLEWHITE
A light, elegant chair with a drop-in seat. The front of the seat often is curved in a serpentine shape. The shield back can be carved or upholstered.

ROUND BACK HEPPLEWHITE
Slim elegant legs without stretcher bars make these unsuitable for rough wear. Hepplewhite chairs also look good in living rooms and bedrooms.

SQUARE ARM ADAM
This square shaped chair has a low back with a carved panel, tapering legs and upholstered seat. Adam furniture is also called neo-classical.

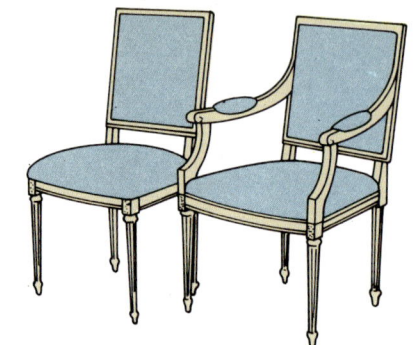

UPHOLSTERED ADAM
The back panel and seat are upholstered and there are sometimes upholstered pads on the carver arms. This style can also make an elegant bedroom or living room chair.

SCROLL ARM REGENCY
The back panel can be elaborately carved or with a simpler design. The seats are upholstered and the curved legs reasonably sturdy without stretcher bars.

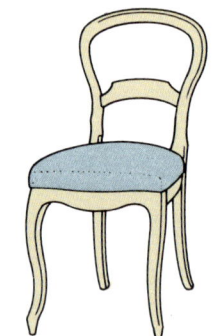

VICTORIAN BUCKLE BACK
The back is curved to fit the body with a rail which can be decorated with carving. The seat is upholstered. Looks good in both formal and informal settings.

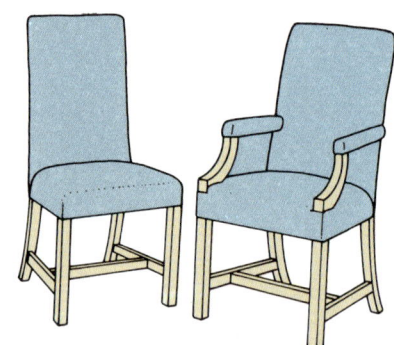

UPHOLSTERED PANEL BACK
Derived from 17th century styles, the fully upholstered back and seat give a solid appearance and shows off boldly-patterned upholstery fabric effectively.

BUTTONED LEATHER PANEL BACK
Similar in appearance to the upholstered panel back but the buttoning allows for a more sculptured back. Solid carver arms give a heavy appearance.

SPINDLE BACK
A country chair with many variations in style. The back is made up of either a single or a double row of spindles and the seat can be wood, rush woven or upholstered.

COMB BACK FARMHOUSE
Developed from the 18th century spindle back chair, the back rail curves to fit the sitter and the seat is moulded. Add squab cushions for extra comfort.

WINDSOR
Styles range from the sturdy to the more finely turned. The back is often supported with two struts for extra strength and the carver arms can continue round the back.

WHEELBACK WINDSOR
A development of the Windsor chair, with the central spindles replaced by a carved splat, often incorporating a wheel. Windsor chairs are made in a range of woods.

BENTWOOD
Simple curved lines made by steaming and bending the wood into shape, with various styles for the back. Usually made from stained beach with a solid or cane seat.

Sideboards and Trolleys

BUFFETS AND TROLLEYS

When guests arrive for dinner they deserve something more than a tray on the lap in front of the television. For special family dinners, or when you're entertaining, you will want to make sure that the meal is easy to serve and keep warm.

Such occasions can cause many different problems. As well as keeping the food hot while it is waiting to be served, you will also need to transport it from the kitchen to the dining room easily – stories of tripping over the cat when holding the results of several hours of cooking are all too common!

SIDEBOARDS

A sideboard kept in the dining room for your best dinner set means things can be kept away from daily usage.

The sideboard (or buffet) has tra-ditionally been used to hold serving dishes and cutlery but it can provide more unorthodox storage in many modern living rooms. A sideboard also provides a good sized surface to rest things on.

Sideboards don't necessarily have to look traditional. There is a wide range of contemporary designs, many allowing you to mix and match the rest of your dining room furniture.

TROLLEYS

Unless you have a serving hatch (or different floor levels), a trolley is quite simply the best way of moving large quantities of food from the kitchen to the dining room. And if space is limited, a folding trolley is a great boon. Trolleys can have two or three shelves and, like sideboards, come in many different designs and materials – wood, metal or plastic, and in both modern and antique styles. Prices vary a great deal too – from a few pounds for a plastic trolley to hundreds for solid wood.

HOTPLATES

Hotplates come in many shapes and sizes and range from trolleys which incorporate a hotplate to individual plate-warming blankets. Some can even be built in to kitchen worktops. The method of using electricity to pass heat through a conducting material such as steel has been familiar in hospital and school kitchens for years. Small, portable hot trays are designed to retain heat while they are carried to the table and usually include a hot spot, with a higher degree of heating capacity for liquids such as soups.

Most trays have detachable leads to enable you to carry them to the table. They are, in the main, designed for fairly short-term heating.

The handles on hotplates should always be of a non-conductive material such as wood, so that they can be carried safely with no risks of burns.

As anyone who makes a habit of eating out will have realised, not all hotplates are powered by electricity. Many restuarants use candles to keep the food hot. Although this method involves lighting the candles and making sure that they don't burn down, it removes the worry of using a flex.

STYLES OF SIDEBOARD

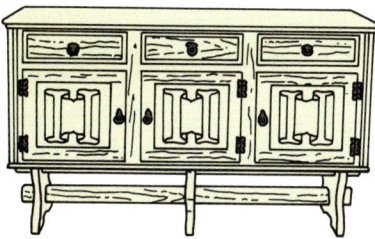

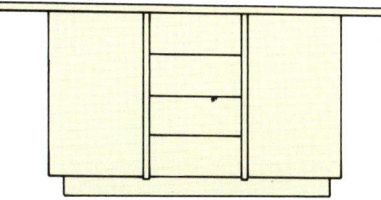

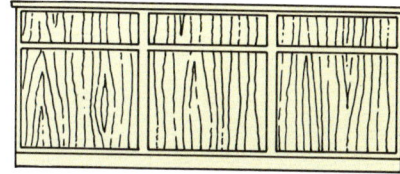

TRADITIONAL SIDEBOARD
Style Traditional solid oak sideboard with three doors and three drawers. Such sideboards usually have shelves inside.
In use More suitable for spacious dining rooms as it takes up a large amount of space.

MODERN SIDEBOARD
Style Beech sideboad with central drawers and cupboards either side. Notice the very modern, streamlined shape.
In use Provides lots of storage in a piece that can be bought to tie in with existing dining room furniture.

CUPBOARD-STYLE SIDEBOARD
Style Sideboard made up of three cupboards topped with drawers. The simple, streamlined shape would best suit a fairly modern room.
In use Provides a large amount of storage space both inside the cupboards and drawers and on the surface.

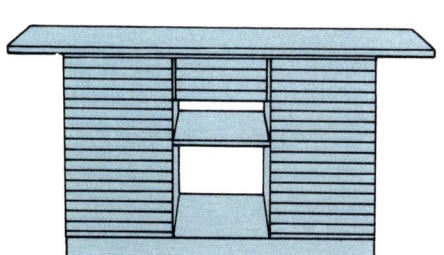

LACQUERED SIDEBOARD
Style Sleek sideboard with a glossy lacquer finish. A range of matching dining room furniture is available with this sideboard.
In use Designed as an attractive piece of furniture rather than a storage unit.

SIDEBOARD AND CABINET
Style Sideboard with two wall-hung cupboards and three floor-standing drawers. A matching glass-fronted cabinet can be used for displaying attractive pieces of china and glass.

STYLES OF TROLLEY

THREE-TIER TROLLEY
Style Three-tier trolley with removable top tray. The frame and tray surrounds are made of anodized aluminium and the trays are heat and stain resistant melamine.
In use Only useful for moving food and china.

FOLDING TROLLEY
Style Two-tier folding trolley which has heat and stain resistant melamine trays. This particular trolley has a simulated marble finish with brass finish aluminium frames.
In use Overcomes storage problems as it is easy to fold away and open out.
Watchpoint Designed for occasional use. Not suitable for transporting heavy loads.

CUPBOARD TROLLEY
Style Two-tier trolley with second shelf formed by the top of the cupboard. Sturdy and stable.
In use Solves both storage and transporting problems simply and efficiently.

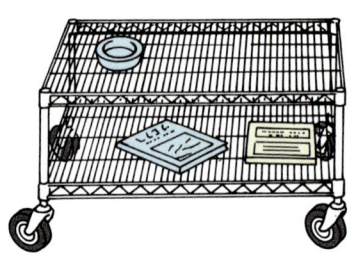

DRINKS TROLLEY
Style In a mahogany finish.
In use Designed with a special section to hold bottles. The bars at the sides stop glasses from sliding off the trolley.

HIGH TECH TROLLEY
Style Metal trolley available with either two or three tiers. This trolley is best suited to an ultra-modern interior.
In use Can be used as a storage unit for the television or video or a trolley.

HOSTESS TROLLEY
Style Food server with sliding top trays, heated cupboard and four two-pint dishes with stainless steel lids. The glass door is heat resistant. There is an unheated bottom shelf for other items that don't need to be kept warm.
In use Ideal for large families or frequent entertaining.

STYLES OF HOTPLATE

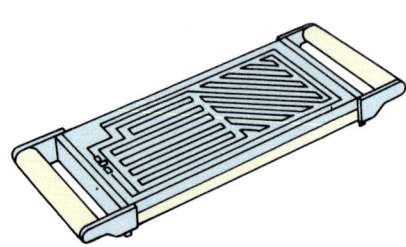

HEATED TRAY
Style Made of toughened glass with teak handles. Has a neon power light and a detachable lead which makes it easier to carry.
In use A heated tray is substantially cheaper than a hostess trolley and can take two or three plates at a time.

CANDLE HOTPLATE
Style Hotplate with metal plate heated by one or two candles that keep the food warm as they gradually burn down.
In use These hotplates can only hold one or two plates at a time and they don't get as hot as an electrically-heated plate.

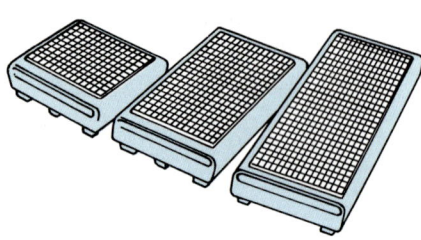

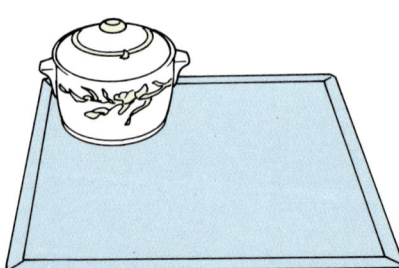

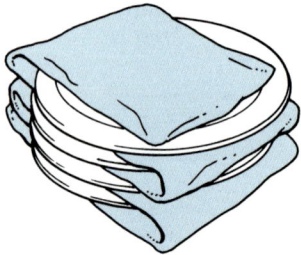

PERFORATED HOTPLATE
Style Candle below a perforated metal tray keeps the food warm. Some candle hot trays have automatic snuffers which make it easier to extinguish the flame.
In use Easy to stack and available in single, double or triple plate sizes. Replacement candles are cheap and easily available.

BUILT-IN HOTPLATE
Style Designed to set into a kitchen worktop. Made of ceramic coated glass with a temperature warning light.
In use Its slimline design means that you don't have to forfeit drawer space and the plate is fully sealed against spillages. Has a hot spot for liquids.

ELECTRIC PLATE BLANKET
Style This is a cheap and space-saving alternative to more expensive hotplates. The blanket wraps around your plates so they are warm when needed.
In use Can heat (and keep warm) up to eight plates at the same time.

Choosing Glassware

Glass is a man-made substance which is the result of a long process of turning different chemicals into a transparent solid at very high temperatures.

There are three groups of glass which are generally used for domestic glassware. Crystal glass contains oxide of lead and has good optical qualities. Lower-priced soda-lime glass – which is based on sand, soda ash and limestone – is a good all-purpose glass, while 'borosilicates' (a mixture of glass and ground stone) are used for cooking utensils and for heavy duty glassware.

Lead glass is sturdy and elegant; the highest quality is known as full lead crystal. This and crystal glass are light materials and are most often used for luxury drinking glasses.

Soda lime glass can be produced by hand or by automatic machine processes; it can be plain or opal coloured. Cut crystal (which is crystal with decorative carvings) is frowned on by wine-lovers, because, they claim, it disguises the wine's colour. And many people believe that the most expensive type is not necessarily the best.

Glassware is made in many different shapes and patterns. If you want a complete set of glassware, simply choose the pattern you like and then buy pieces as you can afford them. But be sure it isn't a fashionable design that will go out of production.

It is always a good idea to shop around first and then choose a design that best complements your china and cutlery – so if both of these are modern, a similar glassware set is best.

CARING FOR GLASS
☐ Wash glasses separately to avoid chipping. Use a plastic bowl or rubber mat in the sink and stand them properly to dry.
☐ Wash glasses in warm soapy water, and avoid abrasive powders; rinse with warm water.
☐ Polish with a soft cloth and store upright: the rim is the most delicate part of the glass.
☐ Clean engraved patterns with a soft brush.
☐ If glasses stick together, pour cold water on the inner glass and hold the outer glass in warm water.
☐ Use a little cooking oil to move sticking decanter stoppers.
☐ Remove lime deposits with tea leaves soaked in vinegar. Other obstinate marks can be shifted by soaking glassware for 24 hours in a strong solution of household detergent and water.
☐ Allow decanters to dry properly before corking – trapped water can smell unpleasant.
☐ Glassware should not usually be cleaned in dishwashers. Valuable crystal, in particular, should always be washed by hand.

STYLES OF GLASSWARE

RED WINE

HOCK

WHITE WINE

CHAMPAGNE FLUTE

CHAMPAGNE SAUCER

WHISKY

BRANDY
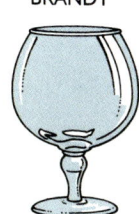

SHERRY

LIQUEUR

RED WINE
Style Glasses for red wine usually hold about 6fl.oz.
In use These glasses are generally used for Burgundy and similar wines, which need space so that they can release their aroma.

WHITE WINE
Style Round-bodied wine glass on a stem for holding 6fl.oz of white wine.
In use Ideal white wine glasses are on a stem; chilled wines can be made tepid if the hand is clamped around the bowl of the glass, and a stemmed glass makes it easier to swirl the liquid about to release its smell.

HOCK
Style Hock glasses traditionally have a long stem. Larger in size than ordinary white wine glasses, but also designed to hold 6fl.oz.
In use Hock glasses are normally used for wines from the Rhine, the Mosel and Alsace.

CHAMPAGNE FLUTE
Style Traditional style, tall champagne glass. Many styles of champagne flutes come in cut or lead crystal: plain glass is unusual as the drink is usually served in something rather elegant. Champagne can also be served in goblet-shaped glasses.
In use These usually hold 5.5fl.oz.

CHAMPAGNE SAUCER
Style Plain saucer-type glass with a wide, shallow bowl that became fashionable in the 1920s. Champagne saucers are not approved of by connoisseurs.
In use Holds 4.5fl.oz.
Watchpoint Storing these glasses needs particular care: ensure plenty of space to avoid chipping.

WHISKY
Style Short tumbler made of uncut, full lead crystal.
In use Whisky glasses are fat, heavy glasses with a thick base. Modern styles are often plain, but many are elaborately cut.

BRANDY
Style Round-bodied, balloon-shaped glass on a short stem. Holds 14fl.oz.
In use The balloon glass allows the warmth of the hand to release the spirit's aroma.
Watchpoint These glasses are not meant to be filled to the brim!

SHERRY
Style A slender glass on a tall stem.
In use Sherry and port glasses should contain no more than about 3fl.oz of wine. True sherry glasses are narrower and taller than port glasses but nowadays many combine the functions of both.

LIQUEUR
Style Long-bodied, tapering glass on a very short stem.
In use Liqueur glasses come in many different sizes but the smallest, designed to hold 2fl.oz, is the most common.

GOBLET
Style Large, round glass on a thick stem. Goblets are thicker and heavier than wine glasses.
In use Goblets can be used to hold many different drinks and make an excellent all-purpose glass.

LONG GLASS
Style Plain, tall glass.
In use These tall glasses are called by the American name Hi-ball.

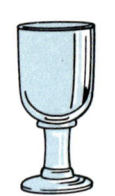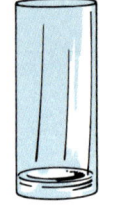

COCKTAIL GLASS
Style Cocktail glass available in plain or patterned glass. Most types of a similar style hold 5fl.oz, while tall cocktail glasses have an 11fl.oz capacity.
In use Cocktail glasses are designed to make mixed drinks with a spirit base. These glasses can nowadays be bought at relatively low prices.

IRISH COFFEE GLASSES
Style Looks rather like a glass mug on a short stem.
In use Used to serve black coffee, with Irish whiskey and double cream.
Watchpoint Glass is generally a poor conductor of heat. When a glass is filled with boiling water the inside heats up and expands, but the outside expands more slowly and the result is a crack. To avoid this, put a spoon in the liquid to draw away the heat.

BEER GLASS
Style Popular shapes are the Straight beer glass. (Pilsener) or the glass tankard. They come in measured ½-pint or pint sizes.

NOVELTY GLASSWARE
Style Novelty, fashion glassware decorated with coloured designs.
In use Suitable for any type of juice or soft drink: a good idea for older children as they tend to be more careful if they have their own favourite glass to use.

WINE DECANTER
Style Wine decanter in full lead crystal – traditional ones are in uncut crystal while the more modern ones are simply plain.
In use Most wine decanters hold 38fl.oz of wine.

SPIRIT DECANTER
Style Square spirit decanter usually

available in cut crystal.
In use This style holds 26fl.oz but there are larger sizes available in the same design.

SHIP'S DECANTER
Style Heavy-bottomed ship's decanter originally designed for use at sea.
In use Holds 35fl.oz.

SHERRY OR PORT DECANTERS
Style Decanter in plain (uncut) lead crystal. These decanters can be used for either drink. The first (left) is rather modern; the second is more traditional and comes in full lead crystal. Holds 28fl.oz.

MAGNUM DECANTER
Style Top of the range, Magnum decanter. As its name implies this holds twice as much as the average sized decanter – 60fl.oz.

ICE BUCKET
Style Uncut, lead crystal ice bucket that comes complete with a pair of stainless steel tongs.
In use Ice buckets can be bought to complement or co-ordinate with a glassware set.

BISCUIT BARREL
Style Full lead crystal biscuit barrel in diamond cut pattern.

In use A glass biscuit barrel is an attractive display container but there are no special benefits to be gained by using glass.

SUGAR AND CREAM SET
Style Set made in lead crystal. This set has interwoven colourways.
In use These sets can be bought to complement your existing glassware.

FRUIT AND SALAD BOWL
Style Fruit and salad bowl with matching dishes in crystal.
In use A set of decorative tableware designed for everyday use at an everyday price.

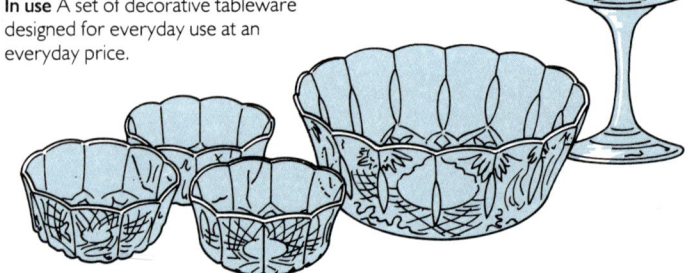

LOW VASE
Style Low vase in ornamental full lead crystal.
In use A piece such as this – at the very top end of the market – is designed for its beauty and ornamental value rather than for heavy use; but sturdiness is part of its high quality.

Choosing China and Ovenware

Buying a set of china can be quite a bewildering experience as there are many different shapes and patterns available to choose from.

And in addition to these different shapes and patterns, crockery is available in different materials too. Porcelain and china are two names for the same thing: clay fired at a very high temperature to produce delicate but strong crockery with a glossy non-porous core.

It's called china, because Chinese potters were working on it as early as the 9th century. It was introduced to Europe by Italian travellers, who described it as 'porcellana', their word for the translucent, smooth, white cowrie shell.

Bone china is a purely British phenomenon, invented in the 18th century by Thomas Frye of Bow, in London's East End. He discovered that adding bone ash to the porcelain clay makes it extra white. It's a technique that's still used today.

Two types of clay are used in today's crockery. Porcelain is made from kaolin or china clay, which is a primary clay. That means it is dug from the ground where it is formed, untainted by other minerals. Secondary clays, like those used in earthenware, have been moved from their source, often by rivers for example, and tend to be tainted with other substances. This can make them more elastic (but less durable). Since impurities reduce strength, bone china is not as strong as porcelain.

Designs, including plate shapes and patterns, vary from manufacturer to manufacturer and range from traditional through to classic and modern styles. No one can really tell you which is the right design for you – that comes down to personal taste. But the most important thing to remember is that the service you choose to collect – few can afford to buy a whole set in one go – will be a lifetime's investment.

Classic shapes and patterns wear better than modern sets. For example, something in cream and purple is not likely to last as long as a plain white plate with a gold border, and there's less risk of manufacturers discontinuing classic styles as fashion changes. If you are unlucky and the manufacturer does stop making your set, they usually give two years' notice. If you're not aware that your service has been discontinued, look in reject china shops for any extra pieces.

Buying a full dinner service is quite an investment, especially if you plump for more expensive china. Generally speaking, you get what you pay for, so the higher the quality of the porcelain or the more bone ash present in bone china, the more expensive the outlay.

Price is also governed by pattern. The cost of hand-painted china – which tends to be most intricate – reflects the time and energies employed by the skilled craftspeople in making it.

Nowadays it is more common for patterns to be applied by screen printing, in which enamelled colours are built up to make a pattern.

Upmarket designs are often 'lifted' by the addition of gold or platinum. Burnished gold is the best quality and is made from an amalgam of brown gold and mercury. It is fired so that the mercury can evaporate and leave a layer of pure gold.

So-called 'bright' gold has a brassier quality and tends to be less durable, so it may be worthwhile paying more in the first place. However, bear in mind that as gold or gilded decoration is fired at a lower temperature than enamelled colours, it does wear away quite quickly, making the service unsuitable for everyday use.

If this huge variety of options is a bit daunting, it may help to know that gourmets often prefer to eat off the plainest and purest white porcelain. They say it's the best setting for any food.

SIZES
Full dinner services often include a confusing amount of similar but variously sized pieces. Plates can come in five sizes, typically 15, 18, 21, 23 and 26cm sizes. The 26cm is the usual dinner plate, 21cm is a dessert plate, and 15cm a side plate. If you prefer a larger side plate the 18cm can be used while the 23cm makes a handy salad plate. Some manufacturers also include a 31cm service plate for use beneath smaller plates.

The shapes and sizes of cups depend on the beverage they contain and meal they're intended for. Generally speaking, a breakfast cup holds 9fl.oz, a tea cup 7fl.oz and a coffee cup 4fl.oz.

Be careful when buying what is described as a 'tea service' as it doesn't include a tea pot, milk jug or sugar bowl. Normally, you get six tea cups and saucers and six side plates.

CHINA STYLES

PLATE SHAPES
Plates come in several different styles but their shapes tend to be fairly uniform and you can expect to find dining plates which are either round, oval, octagonal or with fluted edges. Which plate shape is included in a full china set is the decision of the manufacturer but many offer a choice. Modern, unorthodox china sets are more likely to include some rather unusual shapes. The dining plates shown here all belong to dinnerware sets and, as can be seen, the plate design will also influence the plate shape.

CHINA PATTERNS

Your choice should largely be governed by your personal tastes, your decor, the type of food you are likely to serve and even your personality. Patterns tend to fall into three main categories: traditional, classic and modern. Traditional styles (shown left) tend to be well known and much loved designs – they work equally well as wall plates and often antique styles in the same pattern can be found. Classic patterns (centre) are likely to be the longest lasting as their simplicity means that they won't date easily or clash with food or decor. These styles work well for daily use or as a special dinner service. Modern styles (right) are designed to incorporate the latest fashion trends and for that reason are best for daily or frequent use as the pattern may not be so appealing a few years later.

TEA AND COFFEE SETS

According to your tastes and your needs, you can have a tea or coffee set that matches the rest of your dinnerware, you can have one that is completely different, or you can combine both options and keep one set for special occasions. And as you're likely to use a teaset more often than you use your full dinner set, a different design is sensible for everyday use. The set here has a bold, attractive design and its size make it ideal for breakfast. These sets do vary in size and shape (see those shown in the china and ovenware photographs too). Classic styles (flatter and more oval than the one shown) are available as well, so try to see as many as possible before you choose.

OVENWARE

This china can go straight from the oven to the table so you don't have to worry about putting the food in special serving dishes. If you want dishes that can go on direct heat, look out for sets that are flameproof too. Expect to find casserole, soufflé, flan and gratin dishes, ramekins, platters, soup bowls and plates all available in these services. Materials are usually earthenware and stoneware – either glazed or unglazed. Stoneware is fired at a higher temperature than earthenware, making it harder and a bit more expensive but it is versatile and can go straight from freezer to microwave. Earthenware retains heat and is ideal for slow cooking.

CHINA SETS

Some sets consist of just plates, cups and saucers and sometimes a tea or coffee pot. Such sets are usually low priced and designed to be bought in one go. But a full dinner service should consist of dinner plates, side plates, saucers, casseroles, meat platters, a cake or bread and butter plate, a gravy boat and stand, a soup tureen and soup dishes, an open jug and more often than not, a full tea service too. However, there is no need to collect every single piece from a china set: just what you need. Often manufacturers will include two or three different styles of the same piece as a choice. Modern sets can even have matching cutlery and glassware to give a totally co-ordinated look. However, this option does tend to be at the lower end of the market and is thus more suitable as a set for daily or frequent use.

It is usual to have enough for six people (ie, six plates, bowls, saucers, cups, and so on) but buy more, or less, to suit your needs.

Kitchen Knives and Cutlery

Preparing a meal becomes a much simpler task if you have a selection of knives suitable for cooking. Although there are many different types of kitchen knives available, most people manage with just three or four specialist knives. Look at what's available to see which ones best suit your needs.

Most kitchen knives have stainless steel or carbon steel blades, with a variety of handles, usually black plastic or wood, securely riveted to the blade. Stainless steel is much easier to keep clean, but carbon steel takes a better edge. And as the metal discolours and rusts easily, carbon steel knives should never be left wet. If they are stored and not used for a while, wipe them with olive oil when you are going to use them again.

So long as they are kept well sharpened, plain-edged blades give the smoothest cut; serrated or fluted-edged blades need little or no sharpening, and are also cheaper.

Price is usually an indication of quality. The best kitchen knives are craftsman-made from forged steel, and cannot be cheap. Several excellent ranges come from France and West Germany, as well as Sheffield. Look for a guarantee (this may be for 15, 25 or 50 years), and buy from a specialist cutler or kitchen equipment shop (one which is used by the catering trade).

Blunt knives are not only inefficient but are also potentially dangerous, as applying too much pressure can cause your hand to slip. The traditional tool for use on plain blades is a fine carborundum stone or a sharpening steel. The latter are easier to handle but eventually create a crinkled edge.

In either case it pays to have good knives professionally re-shaped and sharpened from time to time. Knives with fluted or serrated edges may not need any sharpening – or they may require special techniques. Check when buying. Store knives in a knife block or on a magnetic rack to preserve the edges and prevent accidents.

Many different types of kitchen knife are made, and it's important to use the right one. The sizes given below are for the blade, not the whole knife.

PREPARATION KNIVES

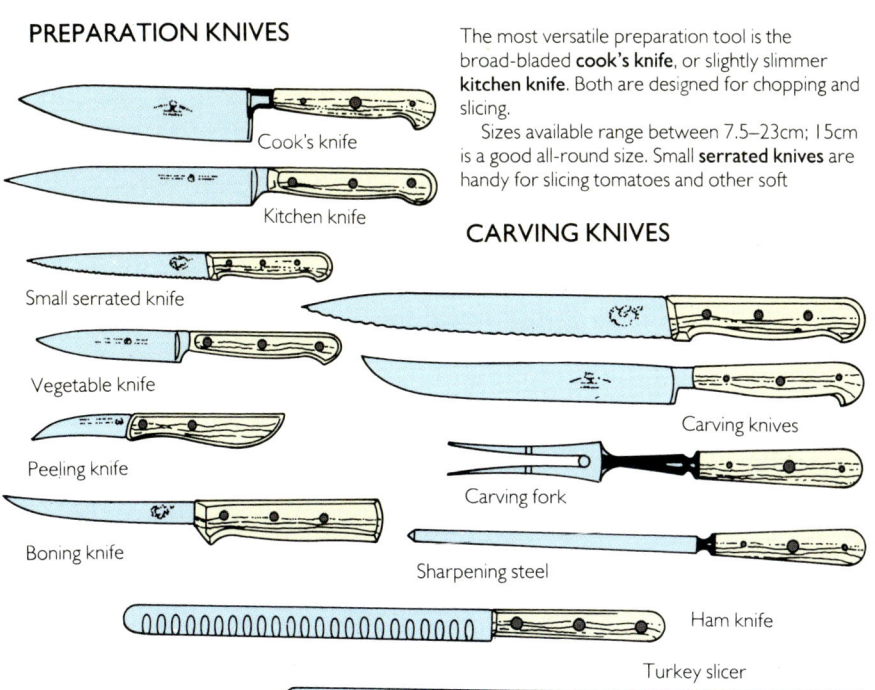

Cook's knife

Kitchen knife

Small serrated knife

Vegetable knife

Peeling knife

Boning knife

CARVING KNIVES

Carving knives

Carving fork

Sharpening steel

Ham knife

Turkey slicer

The most versatile preparation tool is the broad-bladed **cook's knife**, or slightly slimmer **kitchen knife**. Both are designed for chopping and slicing.

Sizes available range between 7.5–23cm; 15cm is a good all-round size. Small **serrated knives** are handy for slicing tomatoes and other soft vegetables thinly, and if they are kept sharp they can double as steak knives.

Do not confuse small cook's knives with **vegetable or paring knives**. The latter are lower quality, and so cheaper, as they are only meant for scraping and peeling. However, if you prefer to buy knives designed for a particular purpose, special **peeling knives** are available too. Blades for these knives can be straight or curved, serrated or plain. Sizes available range from 6–9cm.

Boning knives have narrow blades about 12cm long, designed to slip easily between flesh and bone. Filleting is best done with a special flexible-bladed knife.

CARVING KNIVES

A traditional carving set consists of a **carving knife**, a **twin-pronged carving fork** and a **sharpening steel**. Smaller carving knives are more versatile (particularly useful for filleting) but you really do need a long carving knife if you are going to be able to deal with a large joint neatly and efficiently.

Special carvers with long, round-ended and straight blades are made for slicing ham, salmon and turkey. Small carvers with upward-curving blades are handy for carving and jointing poultry. These knives tend to range from about 18–28 cm in size.

SPECIALIST KNIVES

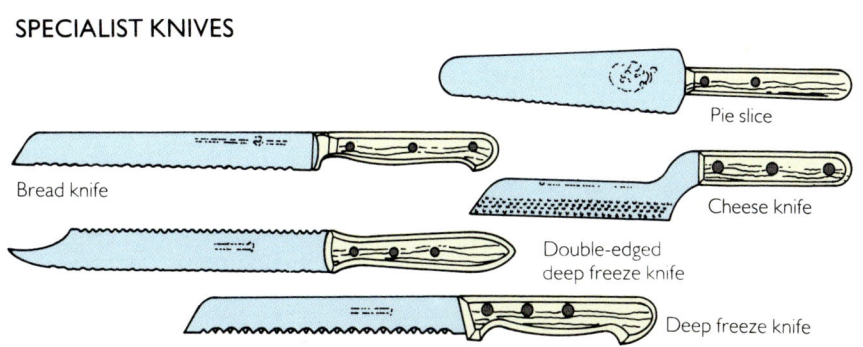

Bread knife

Pie slice

Cheese knife

Double-edged deep freeze knife

Deep freeze knife

A **deep freeze knife** has a strong, coarsely serrated blade for dealing with frozen meat. If you need to carve large quantities of frozen meat, it's sensible to use the right knife – although a carver might seem suitable it could easily be ruined. A **bread knife** is long enough to slice a large loaf, but does not have to be razor sharp; serrated blades are traditional. A combined **pie slice** and spatula is convenient for cutting and serving pastry, but don't use it on non-stick bakeware. For cutting large quantities of cheese use a special **cheese knife** which has an etched blade which prevents the cheese you are cutting from clinging messily to the knife.

CANTEENS OF CUTLERY

A basic set of cutlery consists of seven or eight items making up a place setting: table knife and fork; dessert knife, fork and spoon; soup spoon and teaspoon; sometimes a tablespoon as well. A ten-piece setting consists of the seven basic items plus a fish knife and fork and a coffee spoon. A canteen – a velvet-lined, presentation box or cabinet designed to hold 6–12 place settings – may also include serving spoons and a carving set. Top quality ranges also offer special items such as pastry forks, steak knives and serving pieces in matching patterns.

Cutlery can be bought in four different ways: in a canteen, in gift boxes, by the half-dozen or (cheaper ranges only) by the piece. Canteens are most useful for silverware, as the lined box helps to prevent scratching and tarnishing.

Materials 'Stainless' steel cutlery should really be called 'rust-free', as it is on the Continent; it can stain, but does not tarnish with time like silver plate. The best quality is made from 18/8 Sheffield stainless steel (18 per cent chromium and 8 per cent nickel) and may be guaranteed for up to 50 years. Silver-plated cutlery (electro-plated nickel silver or EPNS) is made from nickel with a thin coating (10–35 microns) of silver. The thickness of the coating affects the price and the length of guarantee, which can range from between 20 and 50 years.

Bronze-plated cutlery was in vogue a few years ago, but proved difficult to keep sparkling; gold-plated cutlery is made, but is naturally extremely expensive. The handles of most traditional cutlery are made from the same metal as the business end, except for designs featuring bone effect or horn handles. Modern designs may have colourful plastic handles or wooden ones featuring brass rivets.

Quality There is a British Standard for cutlery (BS 5577) which applies to both silver plate and stainless steel. But as it is very exacting, only the most expensive ranges conform to it. When buying check that not just the number but also the BSI kite mark is present on every piece, not just forks and spoons (knives are the most difficult to make). A number without a kite mark means that the manufacturer claims to conform to the standard, but his work isn't inspected.

Design Choose a design that complements your dining room styling and china. Elaborate Georgian-style silver-plate will not look its best on stripped pine alongside peasant-style earthenware plates. Conversely, café-style knives and forks are not the thing for an oval mahogany table and a bone china dinner service. If cutlery is to be a gift, and you do not know the setting, pick a classic silver plate design or good quality Scandinavian stainless steel.

CUTLERY STYLES

TRADITIONAL
These designs are based on the work of 18th and early 19th century silversmiths. They tend to be elaborately shaped and patterned.
Materials Silver plate and stainless steel.

CLASSIC
This group includes versions of plain traditional styles such as rattail, which has been popular ever since it first appeared in the reign of Queen Anne. This is the sort of unobtrusive, long-lasting cutlery used in the best hotels. Similar designs may appear under different names.
Materials Silver plate and stainless steel.

TRADITIONAL

CLASSIC

MODERN

CAFÉ STYLE

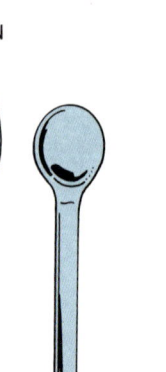

MODERN
Twentieth century cutlery designers have worked in two main ways. Some have applied new patterns to basically traditional shapes. Others have rethought the shapes themselves. Plain, modern shapes are described as Scandinavian.
Materials Mainly stainless steel.

CAFÉ STYLE
A distinct type of modern cutlery, basically French in inspiration. Handles are either shiny, bright plastic or matt black plastic simulating ebonized wood, or wood fixed with rivets.
Materials Stainless steel.
Watchpoint Wooden handles don't like dishwashers.

INDEX

PHOTOGRAPHIC CREDITS
1 IPC Magazines/Robert Harding Syndication, 2-3 IPC Magazines/Robert Harding Syndication, 4-5 IPC Magazines/Robert Harding Syndication, 6 IPC Magazines/Robert Harding Syndication, 9 National Magazine Co/Good Housekeeping, 10-11 Arcaid/Annet Held, 11 EWA/Michael Dunne,12 EWA, 13 EWA/Michael Dunne, 14(t) Richard Paul, 14(bl) Richard Paul, 14(br) Cristal Tiles, 15 EWA/Michael Dunne, 16(t) Dulux, 16(b) Bo Appeltoft, 17(t) National Magazine Co/Good Housekeeping, 17(b) Ken Kirkwood, 18-19 Nathan Ltd, 20(t) Dorma, 20(bl) Crown Paints, 20(br) EWA/Michael Nicholson, 21(tr) Benn Publications, 21(b) EWA/Michael Crockett, 22(tl) Bo Appeltoft, 22(tr) EWA/Michael Dunne, 22(b) Richard Paul, 23 Habitat, 24(l) Swish, 24-25(t) Syndication International, 25(b) EWA/Tim Street-Porter, 26(bl) EWA, 26-27(t) Smallbone of Devizes, 27(b) Junckers, 28(t) EWA/Michael Dunne 28(b) EWA/Neil Lorimer, 29 EWA/Dennis Stone, 30 EWA/Michael Dunne, 31 EWA/Michael Nicholson, 32 EWA/Michael Dunne, 33(t) EWA/Spike Powell, 33(b) EWA/Michael Nicholson, 34(t) Syndication Internation, 34(b) Jean-Paul Bonhommet, 35 Maison Marie Claire/Chabaneix/Peuch, 36-37 Jahres Zeiten Verlag/Peter Adams, 38(b) Perrings, 38-39 Jahres Zeiten Verlag/Peter Adams, 39 PWA International, 40(t) EWA, 40(b) National Magazine Co/Good Housekeeping, 41 National Magazine Co/Good Housekeeping, 42 EWA/Frank Herholdt, 42-43(t) Richard Paul, 43(b) EWA/Spike Powell, 44 National Magazine Co/Good Housekeeping, 45(tl) Di Lewis/Eaglemoss, 45(tr) Jahres Zeiten Verlag/H. J. Dettling, 45(b) EWA, 46(t) Richard Paul, 46(b) IKEA, 47 National Magazine Co/Good Housekeeping, 48(t) EWA/Michael Dunne, 48(b) Arcaid, 49 EWA/Michael Dunne, 50 EWA, 51 Lars Hallen, 52(t) EWA, 52(b) EWA/Michael Dunne, 53 EWA, 54 Jahres Zeiten Verlag/K. Vogel-Berensmann, 55 Jahres Zeiten Verlag/Peter Adams, 56(t) EWA, 56(b) PWA International, 57 Miele Co Ltd, 58-59 EWA, 60 EWA, 61 EWA, 62(t) Camera Press, 62(b) Habitat, 63 EWA, 64 EWA, 65 PWA International, 66 National Magazine Co/Good Housekeeping, 67 MFI, 68 Syndication International, 69 Habitat, 70(t) Syndication International, 70(b) Crown Paints, 71(t) Syndication International, 71(b) EWA, 72 Harrison Drape, 73(t) Harrison Drape, 73(b) Jaycee, 74 Dulux, 75 EWA/Michael Dunne, 76 Habitat, 77(t) Marks and Spencer, 77(b) IKEA, 78(t) Habitat, 78(tr) Habitat, 78(b) EWA/Michael Dunne, 79(t) EWA/Clive Helm, 79(b) Deidi von Schaewen, 80(t) Smallbone of Devizes, 80(b) EWA/Michael Dunne, 91 John Suett/Eaglemoss, 92 John Suett/Eaglemoss.
Front cover: (tl and tr) Old Charm Furniture from Wood Brothers (Furniture) Ltd; (bl) Topaz Collection from Romo Ltd, Nottingham; (br) Eaglemoss/Steve Tanner. (EWA - Elizabeth Whiting and Associates)